DALE HENRY

Also by Dale Henry:

The Proverbial Cracker Jack

To order,
call
1-800-765-6955.

Visit us at
www.AutumnHousePublishing.com
for information on other Autumn House® products.

Are You an Opener?

TEN CANS

DALE HENRY

Autumn House® Publishing
www.autumnhousepublishing.com
A Division of **REVIEW AND HERALD®** PUBLISHING
Since 1861

Published by Autumn House® Publishing, a division of Review and Herald® Publishing, Hagerstown, MD 21741-1119

Autumn House® titles may be purchased in bulk for educational, business, fund-raising, or sales promotional use. For information, please e-mail SpecialMarkets@reviewandherald.com.

Autumn House® Publishing publishes biblically based materials for spiritual, physical, and mental growth and Christian discipleship.

The author assumes full responsibility for the accuracy of all facts and quotations as cited in this book.

Texts credited to NIV are from the *Holy Bible*, *New International Version*. Copyright © 1973, 1978, 1984, International Bible Society. Used by permission of Zondervan Bible Publishers.

This book was
Edited by Jeannette R. Johnson
Cover design by Ron J. Pride
Interior design by Heather Rogers
Cover illustration by Ron J. Pride
Typeset: Garamond Book 11/15

PRINTED IN U.S.A.

12 11 10 09 08   5 4 3 2 1

Library of Congress Cataloging-in-Publication Data

Henry, Dale.
  Ten cans: are you an opener? / Dale Henry.
       p. cm.
1. Leadership—Religious aspects—Christianity. 2. Change (Psychology)—Religious aspects—Christianity. I. Title.
  BV4597.53.L43H46 2007
  253—dc22

                          2007038208

ISBN 978-0-8127-0473-0

To my dad,
Alfred Henry

I miss you.

To my granddaughter,
Kayleigh Peyton Smith

Welcome to the family!

ACKNOWLEDGMENTS

This book was born out of friendship—and frustration. It is a gift to a dear friend and colleague who has endured many hardships and challenges. The book was an accident, really, a way for me to help myself while helping someone else take a step forward when it looked as if all steps led to nowhere.

Greg Little (although he has no way of knowing it) was my catalyst. I would not have explored even my current occupation if he hadn't placed the seed idea in my head. *Ten Cans* is as much his book as it is mine. It was my way of opening both his mind and my own to new possibilities. I hope it has blessed his life as much as his friendship has blessed my life.

Ten Cans is about transition more than change. This is not a book on how to cope with the changes of life; it is a book about how to embrace those transitions. It is a study guide on how to become an opener. I discovered that I have studied openers my whole life—and just didn't know it.

My wife, Debra, is an opener. She taught me about children, and how to be a dad.

My dad, Alfred Henry, became an opener, because he always made me laugh with just his smile.

My mom, Mae Bell Henry, is also a great opener. She taught me how to deal with life's little challenges.

My daughters, LeAnne and Lauren, teach me every day that life makes us openers when we meet the day with joy.

CONTENTS

PREFACE: TEN CANS

Well, here it is.

I know that's a strange way to begin a book, but it's the answer to thousands of kind folks who read my first book, *The Proverbial Cracker Jack*, and asked, "When is your next book going to be available?"

Books are like babies. There's a lot of excitement when your first baby comes along. You sterilize everything, and if a pacifier hits the floor you have to boil water. The camera is always close by, and it seems as if you're always gawking at your newborn. You go into his bedroom and put your hand on his chest to make sure he's breathing.

LeAnne was my first child. Being an only child, I had never been around children, and it caused me to be a little apprehensive. I guess I'd been in too many stores that had that sign: IF YOU BREAK IT, YOU BOUGHT IT! That caused me to sort of shun infants. Of course I had many opportunities to care for babies, but I just waved them off after I had rubbed their heads, and thought, *Seen one, seen them all.*

LeAnne, our firstborn, was a screamer. The nurse didn't ask me if I wanted to hold her; she just plopped her in my arms. I didn't have time to think. I stood very still with the weight of the whole world on my shoulders. I never thought I'd fall in love with a bald-headed, wrinkled, toothless woman, but there she was, and she stole my heart.

The next thing I had to do was tell my wife how absolutely inexperienced I was when it came to infants. Not only had I never held a baby—I had never changed one. I didn't even know how to tell when it was time to change one. I just sort of assumed that a 10-pound diaper held 10 pounds. (I've received a fair amount of chastisement over the years for telling stories on my child bride, Debra June. I don't care what you think of me, but do *not*—I repeat, do *not*—feel sorry for my wife. She gives as good as she gets.)

As I stood trembling before my firstborn, Debra said, "Dale Henry, you have held lots of children." I reminded her that I had allowed folks to put children in my lap, but I had never held one. She looked at me with loving eyes. "All you have to do is pull the elastic leg band loose and stick your finger in there."

OK, I'll admit that I may not be the sharpest tool in the shed, but this did not make sense. I looked at her and said, "What?"

She repeated, "Just pull out the elastic leg band on the diaper and stick your finger in *there!*"

I stopped biting my nails that very day. You get *that* under your nails, and I guarantee that you will not put your fingers in your mouth again.

I became a real baby wrangler, but I always felt like a 6-year-old on Christmas morning every time I checked the diaper. I never quite knew what to expect. "Deb, the baby needs a change." I looked like one of those guys checking the wind before teeing up the ball on the back nine.

Several weeks went by, and we were at my mom and dad's. I wanted to impress them with what kind of dad I was, so I pulled the elastic leg band out and stuck my finger into the diaper.

"What in the world do you think you're doing?" my mom demanded.

"I'm checking this baby's diaper."

"Don't be sticking your finger in there—pull the back of the diaper open and *look* in."

Debra gave me one of those "female" looks, and her face told the whole story. (Ladies, you know it; men, you've seen it.) I will never forget that crooked smile and that feeling of being had.

Well, a first book is something like that—it's a real learning experience. Before you know it, you've stuck your finger into the unknown. The second book? Well, now, that's your second child. Oh, you still love it—it's just more of a been-there-done-that experience. With a second child, when a pacifier hits the floor you stick it in your own mouth and waller it around and say to the baby, "There you go!" No more worries about sanitation or germs. (The really amazing thing is that second babies are usually healthier. Go figure.)

That's how I addressed my second book. The first book had been easy—it just rolled out of my head. My office manager, Michelle, stayed on me, and voilà! It was done. The second book has to be just as good—no, better than your first—or your vendors will say what every writer since Adam has had to hear: "Well, I liked that first one better!"

I'm proud of both of my children, and they turned out to be perfect, although I'll be the first to admit that though this book, like Lauren, is my second "child," it's been a little more challenging than the first book but just as enjoyable. I've had to be my own motivator, and I had to write even when I didn't feel like it.

Someone once asked my grandfather what he fed his dogs. "Turnip greens," he said with a perfectly straight face.

"Frank!" his friend protested. "My dogs won't eat turnip greens."

"Mine wouldn't either—for two weeks," Grandpa replied.

From which I learned that the longer you live, the more you find yourself liking something that was at first a little distasteful.

My mom recently had to have one of those tests that women have to schedule from time to time. Being a guy, I've never been subjected to it; however, according to her account, a mammogram can be compared to having part of your body put in a vise. After her exam, I asked my mom how it went.

"Well," she said, "at first I was a little anxious because a young, very attractive doctor came into the room and began talking to me and asking me all kinds of questions. I thought at first he was there to discuss the test, but after a while it became apparent that he was going to be assisting with the exam. He told me that if I would prefer someone else he would be glad to oblige me. To cut the tension, I said, 'Well, I guess if you've seen one you've pretty much seen them all.'"

"'No, Mrs. Henry,' he replied, 'in my line of work if you've seen one, you pretty much have to see them all.'"

When she chuckled, remembering, I realized where my sense of humor and understanding of transitional behavior came from.

Like my mom's young doctor, I have seen the transitions of life, and my job is to continue to look for them. I hope you'll allow me in to pull out the opener in you by giving you my second book, *Ten Cans: Are You an Opener?*

INTRODUCTION: ARE YOU AN OPENER?

You've heard all the stuff, right?

Embrace change!

Go with the flow!

Stand in one place too long and you'll fall behind!

If you're green, you're growing. And if you're ripe, you rot!

Getting better really means getting better at accepting change. Organizations that create value create their own markets into the future. True change happens when success is achieved in front of the economic curve, not behind it.

This book focuses on the 10 "cans" of change and why our job as leaders is to become the opener.

It is a wonderful day at the Bush bean plant in Tennessee. Ten ordinary cans of chili beans roll off the conveyor belt on their way to a Food City store in Harriman, Tennessee. They arrive and are carefully placed on the shelf.

Ah, there they are! *Now, let's see ... Ten cans should be enough ... No— need to make more than a couple pots,* Deb thinks. She places the cans into the shopping cart and heads for the checkout counter.

At home she unpacks the cans of beans and sets them on the counter in the Henry kitchen. "I just love this new can opener you bought, honey!" she calls to me. "It zips right through the can and doesn't leave that sharp edge the way our old one did."

"What's that, sweetie?" I can barely hear her above the blare of the TV.

"Oh, I was just talking about the new can opener. I love it!"

I walk into the kitchen. In my best W. C. Fields voice I say, "Yes, my love; tools are my life ... What'cha doin'?"

"Making two pots of chili for this weekend's Sunday picnic. Would you take out the trash?"

"You betcha." Grabbing the trash, I pause. "I'm a little worried about Greg."

"Why? I thought you guys had fun playing golf this week."

"Well, his dad isn't doing well. I need to get his name on the prayer list at church."

"Why don't you write him a letter?" Deb suggests.

"You mean an e-mail?"

"No; I mean a letter. It always cheers me up when I get a letter from a friend."

"Good idea," I agree.

Later, when the chili is finished and the dishes are put away, we go to bed, and Debra quickly falls asleep. But I am restless. Unfinished business is a terrible bed partner. I finally doze off with Greg on my mind—then am wide awake with an idea.

I get up and dig the empty bean cans out of the trash. I wash them off and remove the labels. Carefully replacing the lids, I put the cans in a box on the counter, then bound upstairs to the computer.

I write 10 stories and carefully insert one story into each can. The 10 cans are sealed shut, boxed up, and sent to Greg's home the next day.

It's a hot, humid day in Pearl, Mississippi. Greg slides his feet off the bed and scratches his head. *Another day, another dollar— Wait! How does that go? Another day, another dollar; 10 days, 10 dollars; 10 dollars, one drunk; one drunk, 10 days.* He chuckles as he walks to the kitchen for his morning coffee. *Oh, man! I've got to call about Dad …*

"Hey, Mom … Dad's not better? I'll take off work and be there this afternoon … Love you too."

He gets dressed and opens the garage. *What's this? Hey! It's a box from Dale. I wonder what that rascal is up to—probably wants to rub it in that he beat me at golf last week.*

He picks up the box and sets it in the house, deciding to open it later, and jumps in his car and heads for his mom and dad's house.

The next two days are a blur. His father's death, the arrangements, the funeral—the days have taken their toll.

The next morning Greg gets up and shuffles out through the garage for the paper. *Hey! Dale's box. I almost forgot.* Over hot coffee he opens the box and reads the note sitting on top:

Greg, there are 10 cans in this box. Each can tells a story (you know how much I love stories). For the next 10 days, please open one can a day, the first thing in the morning, and read the story that's inside the can. Then e-mail me each night and tell me what you think.

Like all my stories, Greg, they have a beginning—but the end is up to you!

Confused but interested, Greg opens can 1.

CAN OPENER **1**

MY BIGGEST ASSET:

MY LITTLE DEPENDENTS ("... AND FOUR TO GO")

> **Ye have compassed this mountain long enough; turn you northward.** —*DEUTERONOMY 2:3.*

> **You have sized up the mountain long enough; time to climb it and get 'er done.** —*DALE HENRY, LOOSE TRANSLATION.*

Good morning, Greg!

Every Father's Day my kids take me somewhere. Oh, it's nowhere *I* want to go—it's somewhere *they* want to go. And every year I ask Debra why she doesn't go on the Father's Day trip. She always looks at me and says, "'Cause you aren't my daddy."

After church the girls throw some things in the back of the car, and we get in. With my older daughter, LeAnne, in the front and Lauren in the back, the instructions begin: "Turn here, Dad . . . Now, turn here!"

And the next thing I know, I'm in the middle of Pigeon Forge, Tennessee.

"Turn in here, Dad."

It's a place called Ogle's Water Park. *A water park!* If you've been to any water park you've been to Ogle's. I start to think that this could be a cool Father's Day. Splashing around with my girls will be a lot of fun.

LeAnne walks around the car, opens my door, and says, "Daddy, have you ever bungee jumped before?"

The only word that bothers me is the word "before," which means you have never done it before but you are getting ready to. Looking LeAnne right in the eye I reply, "Sweetie, Daddy didn't get to this ripe old age by jumping off perfectly good buildings. It's not happening on Father's Day."

Greg, do you think your kids listen to you? No? Well, believe me, they listen—and watch everything you do. Do you remember what you thought you knew when you were 18 years old? (Everything.) Do you remember what you thought your dad knew when you were 18 years old? (Nothing.) If someone had asked you who you wanted to be like when you grew up, the last person on that list would have been who? (Your dad.)

How old were you, Greg, when you noticed that you were shaving your dad's face? (In other words, we have become our fathers.)

I've always taught my girls not to be quitters. And now they are looking up at me with those puppy dog eyes, and they say, "Are you a quitter, Dad?"

OK. For once in my life I want to say, "Yes, today Daddy is a quitter!" Instead I bend down and say, "Girls, there will be times I will probably let you down. There will be times Daddy is going to be somewhere else when he promised that he would be with you. Sometimes I am going to be late, and I will disappoint you. I'm human. But there is one thing you can count on: I'm not a quitter. *Let's go bungee jumping!*"

We pay our money and walk up the 375 steps to the top of that 180-foot tower. (Oh, yeah. I counted every one of those steps.)

At the top Lauren looks at me and says, "Daddy, is it OK if I go first?"

I say, "Knock yourself out."

She puts on all the apparatus and is checked for safety. She does not turn to her sister, stick out her tongue, and say, "Nyeh, nyeh! I'm going first." She does not look at me and say, "Dad, I will see you at the bottom."

She just jumps.

She jumped 180 feet as if she were jumping off the front porch. I ease over to the handrail and grab it tightly. Looking over the edge, I see my 8-year-old sliding off a big air cushion. I turn to LeAnne. "When we get home," I say, "she gets tested. No one jumps off a 180-foot tower without thinking about it."

LeAnne gives me a searching look. "Dad, do you want to go next—or do you want me to?"

"Baby," I say, "your daddy is a Southerner, and Southern gentlemen always let ladies go first."

So she puts on her apparatus, walks to the handrail, and hangs her toes over the edge. I think, *Oh, my goodness! It runs in the family, mother's side.* However, the longer she stands there, the more she slides her feet back.

Greg, you know what this is all about. How many times has she heard "Don't stand too close to the edge—you might fall"? We adults hear it in other ways: "You can't do that!" "We have tried that before." "You are too old to change jobs." "You aren't going back to school now, are you?" These people are your friends. They love you. They want you to stay the same, be the same, smell the same, and act the same. Same is good; change and transition are bad.

The fellow who's operating the bungee operation says, "Normally, what we do is count backward from five to one, and when you're ready you can jump."

"OK," LeAnne says.

"Five, four, three, two, one . . . "

LeAnne is still there.

"Didn't you hear what I said?" the operator demands.

"I heard you perfectly," LeAnne says stiffly. "You said you were going to count from five to one, and when I was ready I could jump. I'm not ready."

I love to be with my children when they face the dragons of change. I want to comfort them, and help them. We parents want the best for our kids, don't we, Greg? But we can't always be there. So we must teach them while we can to respect and embrace new possibilities. You know what it's like to make a tough decision. I'm not talking about knowing right from wrong; I'm talking about commitment. Decisions are tough, because we will be held accountable.

I look at my daughter huddled on the edge. "LeAnne," I say in a calm, soft voice.

"Yes, Daddy?"

"Honey, you are standing at the edge of a decision, and from where your dad is standing it looks as if you have two choices. You can take one step and enjoy the ride (after all, that's why we're up here), or you can take off all that stuff and walk down the 375 steps that brought you up here. Either way, you'll get to your final objective—the ground. LeAnne, I know why you will not take the steps. There is a little girl down there—your baby sister—and she will chastise you. She will tease you. You will be 90 years old and shuffling down the road, and she still will be saying *buck, buck, buck,* and flapping her arms like a chicken.

"I want you to listen to me, honey, and I want you to listen good: *That will not happen!* I WILL WALK DOWN WITH YOU!" I offer hopefully. I think I'm pretty smart.

Well, she jumped. And now it's my turn.

The bungee guy says, "How do you want to go?"

"I prefer the steps," I say.

He shakes his head woefully. "Mister, mister! Jumping off of this bungee tower is safer than walking on the streets of Pigeon Forge."

I look square at him and ask, "So how many times have you jumped off this thing?"

His voice rises a couple notches. "Personally, I've never jumped."

Sound familiar, Greg? How many times have you been in the middle of a tough decision and someone says, "Oh, I know what I'd do; I know how I'd handle that situation. I'll tell you how I'd react if I were in your shoes." It's easy to make decisions for others because there's no commitment or involvement.

I walk to the edge. I would love to tell you that I jumped like Lauren, and just did it. I would love to tell you that I jumped like LeAnne, slow and thoughtful. I would love to tell you I jumped. Oh, I tried!

Finally, I decide I will lean out. You can lean out only so far, and then you'll fall. (Have you ever seen those cartoon characters who can lean way out, then come back? I can do that. I have some real toe control.) Then I lean out too far and I fall.

Greg, remember that tough decision we've been discussing? Sooner or later you're going to lean over and whisper into someone's ear, "This is what I'm going to do." (Why is it we always tell someone who's going to tell everyone we know?) And the second those words leave your lips your brain says,

"Well, you should have thought about that another minute or two."

The second my feet leave the platform my brain says, "So, Dale, if you lose control of bodily function, headfirst might not have been a real good idea."

I don't lose control of bodily function, and I slide off that big air cushion and spend the rest of the day splashing in the water park with my girls.

All day long at the water park LeAnne keeps reciting that childhood mantra "One for the money, two for the show, three to get ready, and four to go." I can't tell you the exact moment it happens, the moment when truth and realization come to conscious understanding, but I had forgotten the importance of "four to go." The significance of commitment begins when you open your life to transition.

At home again LeAnne and Lauren ask, "How was your Father's Day trip, Daddy?"

"It was great!" I say.

LeAnne looks up with a twisted smile. "No, Dad; on a scale of one to five."

"Sweetie, it was a 'four to go!'"

Greg puts the story down.

Lots of things are zooming through his mind. He reviews decisions that he has put off during the past few months about work and his personal life. The rest of the day flies by as he makes a list of things that need his attention. He has all his "four to go's" prioritized, and has a new understanding of the route he's going to take as he climbs his personal mountain. That evening he sends an e-mail to Dale:

Thanks for the encouragement, friend! I enjoyed the first can—it couldn't have arrived at a more perfect moment. You're right—"four to go" is a problem for me, too. I guess I've done it for so long that it seems natural. Dad's passing and your gift both have made me see that I must be an opener for those who are important to me.

You asked me to tell you what I think. I think openers find avenues where others find dead ends. As you know, Dale, I've been putting off a very tough decision about my career. LeAnne and Lauren have taught me that standing in one spot only keeps the grass from growing. I'm going to seek wise counsel from one of our mentors. I believe God has some interesting transitions for me. Talk to you tomorrow. Keep me in your prayers.

Your brother, Greg

CAN OPENER

OUR BIGGEST COMMITMENT:
RELATIONSHIPS (NOT ALL WILL SLEEP,
BUT ALL WILL BE CHANGED)

Listen, I tell you a mystery: We will not all sleep, but we will all be changed.—*1 CORINTHIANS 15:51, NIV.*

Let me tell you a secret: Wake up and smell the coffee! Only God can change people.—*DALE HENRY, LOOSE TRANSLATION.*

The next morning Greg jumps out of bed with new hope. His feet are no longer shuffling along; they are gliding. He is a man with a purpose! He reviews his four-to-go list and begins getting ready for church. As he showers, he notices that he has a smile on his face.

He's been through some faith-bending events that have caused him to question his relationship with God. An accident as a teen put him in a coma and robbed him of memory. While working on his doctorate he lost his youngest child suddenly and tragically. This horrific loss put a strain on his already-weakened relationship with his wife. Years later this stress resulted in a separation and divorce that Greg still has trouble dealing with. His son became distant, and Greg has continued his downward spiral by working in a dead-end job he has never liked.

Despite these setbacks, this morning Greg is a man on a mission. Stepping from the shower, he prepares physically and mentally to worship. He's having an open dialog with a Friend he has somehow neglected—he's once again talking to God on the mountain. Instead of carrying his burdens, he has starting sharing them.

He opens can 2 and begins to read.

Greg, there's a little sign over the door of the infant department at my church, a quote from Scripture that is certainly appropriate in that setting: "Not all will sleep—but all will be changed!"

I'd like to offer a slight twist on these wise words that might meet our needs better: Don't get caught napping, because transitions are everywhere. One of my favorite commercials is the one that has the guy asking his wife what a certain light switch controls in their house. He rapidly switches it on and off while saying, "OK; on–off–on–off. See anything?" Meanwhile, a garage door down the street is opening and closing on the hood of a hapless woman's car.

Have you ever wondered what outcomes are put into place because of our own actions? I am so blessed that I have a visual memory. I can close my eyes and play back events from my life like a video recorder. Deb and I (if the good Lord is willing) will celebrate our thirty-fourth wedding anniversary this coming October. I can still see that day...

Debra and I got married in the Laurel Bank Missionary Baptist Church in Friendsville, Tennessee. The ceremony was simple but beautiful. My mom and dad sat on the front pew on the right, and Deb's mother sat to the left. They all looked so happy! Debra's uncle Bob escorted her down the aisle (her father had passed away tragically several years earlier) and placed her hand in mine. It was so warm! I remember turning and my dad winking at me, and that feeling of joy still flows over me like a waterfall.

When we turned to face the congregation at the end of the ceremony, the pastor announced, "Ladies and gentlemen, may I introduce Mr. and Mrs. Debra Field!" (I don't know; maybe he was right!) Then we ran out of the church. (I'm not sure why Deb was running, but I had my own reasons.) We burst out of the church and onto the front porch—and there stood my dad. I couldn't figure out how he could have gotten there before us.

He looked me in the eye and asked, "Can I have a minute of your time?"

To be honest, I wanted to say, "Dad, I'm a little focused right now. Can we talk later?" But I didn't, of course. Instead I said, "You can have all the time you want!"

So he asked Deb if he could borrow me for a minute, and she told him to take all the time he needed and went down to talk to her friends who were getting ready to throw rice at us. (We don't throw rice anymore [it kills the birds]; we throw birdseed—and now we have obese birds.)

My dad put his arms around me. "Son," he said, "you are always going to be my son, but a couple of minutes ago our relationship changed. Until then I could tell you what to do, and you, being a good son, would do whatever I asked. But that has all changed now! Oh, you're still going to be told what to do—it just won't be me who's doing the telling. Could I ask for a couple favors?"

"Sure, Dad; you name it."

"You're going to go on your honeymoon, and when you get back life will get busy. You'll go to work and school, and other things will occupy your time—shopping, mowing, getting the mail, and a million other tasks. These things will take you from your home. Favor number one has to do with you coming back across your threshold and into your house. Every time you come into your house, no matter how many times you leave, always hunt down your wife and tell her that you love her."

"I can do that, Dad."

"Now for my second request. No matter where you find yourself, no matter who you are talking to or what the subject may be, tell everyone how much you love your wife."

"Dad, I understand why I need to tell Deb that I love her, but why do I have to tell everyone else?"

"Because they will talk to her, son."

When we speak well of people, it gets around. Ask any businessperson which is better: to have a customer tell you they appreciate you or to have someone you have never met walk up and say that because his good friend does business with you and thinks highly of you, he too would like to do business with you. Direct appreciation is good, but indirect appreciation is wonderful.

When I share this concept with people, they often say, "That's well and good, but you don't know the people I work with, Dale. You don't know my customers. And you certainly don't know my boss!" What a cop-out! What they are really saying is that it sounds good for someone else; they just don't think it applies to their situation. After I finish a presentation, I think it's hilarious that at least 10 or 15 people will come up to me and dramatically say, "I wish the people I worked with had been here—they really need this!" I'm thinking to myself, *Yeah! I'm pretty sure that's why they sent* you!

A friend once told me that his wife was his friend and that he was happily married. Remember our Scripture text at the beginning of this chapter that says that not all will sleep, but all will be changed? After some review it came to me that what my friend was saying might not have been 100 percent accurate.

For example, let's say you are on the road with me and we arrive on a late flight at McGhee Tyson Airport in Knoxville around 2:00 a.m. We go out of the terminal to my car and jump in. As we're backing up, we feel that unmistakable bumping that means a flat tire. Before we left on this trip we'd had a flat tire, and my wife said that I should have it fixed immediately.

I didn't. Now we're going to call my wife. When she answers the phone, I'll explain that we have a flat tire and tell her how much I would appreciate it if she would come and get us at the airport. Get ready, because Debra is going to say the following: "If you had gotten that tire fixed on Wednesday like I told you to, you would not be at the airport stuck with a flat tire."

In such a situation, your wife is not your friend. Dennis is my friend. He would come and get us pronto—no questions, no comments. He's not married.

Oh, and that happy part. You know—happy wife, happy life. I still try to date my wife. (I'm almost positive that every man since time began married UP.) Like many married men, I have figured out that in relationships with women you can be right or you can be happy—but you can't be both. So I date my wife.

On one of our recent dates we were driving home from one of our favorite restaurants and drove over an overpass. On the other side stood a man holding a cardboard sign: WILL WORK FOR FOOD! Now, I do strange things with the money I keep in my pockets. I keep unbroken bills, such as twenties, in my left pocket, and smaller bills in my right pocket. Without even looking, I reached into my right pocket and pulled out a $10 bill. I rolled down the window and gave the man the money, saying, "I don't know what brought you here and I don't know where you're going, but would you get a hot meal tonight?"

After I rolled up the window, Debra decided that I needed a lesson in dealing with a con artist. She began by telling me that the man would probably use that money to buy alcohol or drugs. Then she regaled me on the economics of being conned: "Ten people giving $10 in one hour is $100 an hour. Not too bad for a little handmade sign, huh?" Pause. Then: "That's all I have to say about that." I have a wonderful wife, but when Deb says, "That is all I have to say about that," it never is. And she immediately cranked right back up again.

After two or three cycles she finally sighed. That was my cue. The sigh meant she was finished, and the discussion was closed. I said, "Now, Debra—"

"Dale Henry, if you think you can make something positive out of this—"

I stopped her in midsentence. "Excuse me, but didn't you sigh?"

"Go ahead," she said.

So I asked Deb the same question I ask everyone who gets caught up in trying to sleep through relationship transitions: "Will I be judged by what I do, or will I be judged by what others do?"

It is the ultimate cop-out. If I don't do anything, then I will be innocent. Doing nothing does not make us innocent; it makes us asleep, dead, unchanged, callous, uncaring, and guilty. Openers stay connected to life by first taking charge of their own transitions and actions. Then they help others around them to become connected as well. In 34 years Deb and I have learned a lot about the give-and-take of relationships. Neither of us is always right, and not often are both of us wrong. You might say that on that wedding day more than a quarter century ago we made more that an exchange of vows. (After all, the most significant question at the wedding is Do you take this woman?) We gave each other our love.

And I'm still crossing the threshold and looking for Deb.

Greg, you might not always sleep, but I guarantee that you will be changed by relationship transitions.

Greg gets up from his computer desk and walks to his bedroom. Standing at the mirror, he pulls a tie from his closet. As he ties his tie, he thinks about the relationships in his life. He lowers his head and begins to pray.

"Dear God, here I stand. I am a man, God, and without You I will remain just a man. Lord, please come into my life; heal me and transition me. Help me to change, this day, for the better. Wash over me, Jesus, and forgive me where I have fallen short. Without You in my life I am nothing; I am lost. Dwell inside me, Holy Spirit, and find within me Your house of worship. Amen."

He looks up, and a feeling of "clean" comes over him that he has not experienced in a long time. Releasing the tie from his fingers, he lets it falls to his chest, half tied. He can't wait until evening—he goes to his computer, logs on, and begins to type:

Dale, it is a little before 10:30 in the morning. I know you and your family are probably at church or heading there right now, but I couldn't wait until evening to tell you about what I learned today. Dale, I've been asleep. I'm not sure when or how long I've slept, but today you helped me realize I've been putting the blame for everything in my life on other people. They don't need changing or transitioning—I do. I have rededicated my life just now. I wanted you to know. I realize you won't read this until later—it just makes me feel good to share it with you. Thanks for your gift.

Your wide-awake brother,
Greg

Greg logs off the computer and grabs his Bible as he heads for the door. Today is not only worship day—it is celebration day as he begins to see the power of the can.

He has a wonderful day. He's with people who want to be better. Christians want to be an example, and it's easy in church. Church is a haven, a place he can feel safe in his worship.

But be careful—the next day is coming!

CAN OPENER 3

MY GREATEST GIFT:
A BETTER ME (BLESS YOUR HEART)

Let all those that put their trust in thee rejoice.—*PSALM 5:11.*

Don't worry; be happy—smile!—*DALE HENRY, LOOSE TRANSLATION.*

Greg jumps up and quickly grabs the third can. Opening it, he reads the story with the enthusiasm of a child.

Good morning, Greg!

You know what? I love being from the South! The whole Southern experience is a blast. And I love Southern phrases. My personal favorite is "bless your heart!" Some of my non-Southern friends will read this and not understand the true meaning of this truly classic phrase, which really means "that's pretty stupid."

You have to use it in context. A Southerner, listening to someone explain how he broke his leg while showing his 3-year-old how easy it is to ride a skateboard, will smile and say, "Bless your heart!" Or when a friend says that he has met the "perfect mate," a Southerner will take one look at that person, recognize her for the nightmare she really is, and smile and say, "Bless your heart!"

The perfect time of my life was high school. That's right! I had tons of friends, and that's when I discovered the most wonderful thing ever invented: GIRLS! And not just plain girls—*Southern* girls. I love it when Southern girls say, "Kaaaaaaaaawwwiiiiiiiiiiiiiiiit!" (That's "quit" to the rest of the world.) By the time they finish saying it, you can go from holding their hand . . . to putting your arm around them . . . to stealing a kiss. Because it takes them forever to get the word out, most Southern boys are done by the time they finish.

I decided early in life that if I was going to settle down and get married, it might as well be with a Southern girl. After all, my mom was a Southern girl, and she was all right. My grandmother was a Southern girl and, like my mom, boy, could she cook! So I made my decision that since I could marry anyone I chose, she would be from the South.

Thereafter, I asked every girl I met a qualifying question: "Where are you from?" Now, everyone on the planet knows that when someone asks you where you're from, you respond by telling them where you were born. One day I asked this pretty little girl I was dating where she was from. She batted her eyelashes (which is the first thing a Southern mother teaches her daughters) and said, "I'm from Macon, Georgia."

It doesn't get any more Southern than Macon, Georgia. So I immediately moved her to the top of my list. (Because of that, and her daddy had a little money.) One thing led to another, and we ended up getting married. As we were driving from the wedding to begin our honeymoon, my wife of less than 15 minutes looked around at the area we were driving through and remarked, "This reminds me of where I was born in Rancho Cucamonga, California!"

Stunned, I gasped, "*What?*"

"This reminds me of where I was born in Rancho Cucamonga, California," she repeated sweetly.

I could not believe my ears.

Well, I've been married to that California woman for almost 34 years now, but California people are just a little different. Oh, don't get me wrong—I like them just fine, but whenever I meet someone from there I always say, "Bless your heart!" And Deb is a little different too. Not in huge ways—just a little different. Let me illustrate.

I'm a runner. I know that whenever I say I'm a runner people will look at me a little funny (you know, like I'm from California), and they think, *He must be healthy; he probably eats healthfully.* Listen. I'm from the South, where gravy isn't just gravy—it's a beverage. I *love* to eat, and when you love to eat and you are five feet six inches tall, you had better run or you'll roll.

Debra doesn't run; she diets. Her favorite thing is salad. Why? It doesn't taste good with gravy. The largest, fattest animal on the planet is the elephant. And what does the elephant eat? You guessed it—salad. The second biggest, fattest animal is the hippopotamus. It eats salad as well. On the other hand, the meanest, leanest, fastest animal is the cheetah. What does the cheetah eat? It sure ain't salad! So if we want to lose weight, maybe we should all eat cheetah.

My real problem with dieting, though, is that people on a diet want *everyone* to be on a diet. When Debra orders a salad, she points to me and adds, "And he will take a salad too." I've been on every diet there is because Debra has been on every diet there is. I was on that fiber diet for a couple of weeks. I hated it. Two weeks on that diet and you start passing wicker furniture. So instead of dieting, I run.

After running one day, I came home hungry to find that Debra was gone, probably to do something with the girls. I hate eating by myself, and I hate going to a restaurant and telling the host that I'm alone. It makes me look pitiful. So I got in the car and drove to Hardee's, my favorite eating establishment. They have great gravy. Most people use the drive-up window to get their biscuits. I don't; I go inside, because you know who's sitting inside Hardee's in a small Southern town at 8:00 in the morning on a workday? No, they're not *old* people; they're *experienced* people, and if you want to learn stuff, you hang around experienced people.

I walked into Hardee's and stepped up to the counter. As I was waiting to give my order, a rather large man came in, probably six feet nine to six feet ten, around 400 pounds. A mountain of a man. I like to look at people and try to guess what they do for a living, and since he was wearing coveralls with the sleeves cut off, I ruled out physician. He had a tattoo on one arm and cigarettes rolled up in the sleeve of his T-shirt. Definitely a truck driver, I decided. The fact that he crawled out of a Roadway truck tilted me toward that conclusion.

He fell into line behind me at the counter, but he was a skoosh too close ("skoosh" is Southern for "I can feel his body heat"), not realizing that his girth was spilling into my personal space. I took a half step forward. He thought the line was moving and also took a step forward, so we're still in the same situation. On top of that, he was a breather, muttering to himself, "What do I want? . . . *Whew!*" With each exhale he was taking the curl out of my hair.

After what seemed an eternity he tapped me on the shoulder. His belt buckle was four inches above my head, so spinning around wasn't an option. I stepped to the side and tipped my head way back. He looked down at me and said in a very Southern accent, "You hongry?"

"Sure!" I said.

He looked all around. "Well, can *you* see me?"

"You betcha!" I assured him, my head still at a right angle to my body. "I can see you."

"Well," he said, "I can see *you,* and I can see *them,*" gesturing toward the waiters. "Why can't they see *us?*"

What this guy was saying was simple: We have the dollar, and they have the biscuit. Let's do the deal! From time to time I can be a man of action, especially if I have a 400-pound hungry man breathing down my neck. I spied a waiter walking by with a big bag of biscuits. (It was easy to tell they were biscuits because of the multiple grease stains on the napkin that covered them.) I caught her in midstride and called out, "Ma'am! Ma'am! Excuse me, ma'am!"

Now, Greg, I'd like to stop the story for a reality check. If you are walking down the street in the South, someone will most certainly stop you and shake your hand.

"How are you doing? Great! What's your name?"

"Greg."

"What's your last name, Greg?"

"Little."

"Who's your daddy?"

Southern people don't want to know just your name; they want to know you. We invented Southern hospitality, after all. We invented "Ya'll come back now, ya hear?"

Well, this waiter turned to me and said, "Can't you see I'm busy?"

I didn't know what to say. "Did you hear what that waiter said to us?" I asked Mountain Man.

"Yeah!" he said. "We ain't gettin' no biscuit."

"Friend," I contradicted, "we are going to get us a biscuit because this is an economy, and in an economy there are two groups of people. You have people who are trying to buy some goods or a service, and you have people who are trying to sell some goods or a service. And when those two groups of people get together, it's a beautiful thing. Now when you pulled off Interstate 40 this morning to get you a biscuit, did you see the marquee out front of the Harriman Hardee's?"

"No, I can't say that I did," he admitted.

"Well, my friend, right out there on the Hardee's marquee it says 'Sausage and biscuit, 79 cents.' And across the street on the McDonald's marquee it says 'Sausage and biscuit, 89 cents.' What that waiter really said to you and to me just now was that *we aren't worth a dime!*"

Now, Greg, here comes a couple questions I'd like to ask. You'll not mind the first question, but the second one will be a bit more difficult:

Have you ever been treated as if you weren't worth a dime? I'll bet you said, "Sure!"

Have you ever treated someone else as if they weren't worth a dime? That's a tough one, but I'll bet you said, "Sure," again. Brother, we all have.

How long has it been since you had an eye exam? Remember all those crazy tests? I especially hate that little poof of air thing. At my last exam the doctor didn't tell me it was coming, and when I jumped he asked, "Did that scare you?" So I got up and said, "I don't know," and I poofed *in his eye. "You tell me—did it scare* you*?"*

Next, he pushes that big round contraption in front of my face and asks, "Which is better, this one or that one?" (The whole thing is rigged, Greg; he knows which one you're going to choose. He takes all that data from the other tests, and the fix is in. This part of the exam is about selling you glasses. If you don't believe me, select the fuzziest image sometime. The doctor will stare you right in the eye and demand, "Now let's look at that one more time.")

Which is better—this one or that one? It's a great question. Let's try it out:

Do you like to be around optimistic people or pessimistic people? Optimistic people, right? Do you like problem solvers or problem causers? Problem solvers, right? How about happy people or constipated people—which one is your favorite?

Just as the eye doctor did, I'm afraid I fixed this little test. We all *want to be optimistic, problem-solving, happy people, right? OK, Greg, I have to ask my final question: If we all want to be optimistic, problem-solving, happy people—then why aren't we? We walk around work saying we love our job, all the while looking as if we've just lost our best friend. If we love our job, maybe we need to notify our face. Saying we love something while looking as if we were weaned on a pickle just doesn't make sense. We want stuff from others that we aren't willing to give. Sure, I want all of that, but only if I can whine. Bless your heart!*

Greg chuckles and gets dressed for work. He can hardly wait to tackle the day with his newfound enthusiasm and energy. He pulls into work and realizes that it's the same place he left a few days ago—the same people with the same negative conversations. He begins to slip into his old skin as he walks into his office and gets online. He logs in and sends a message to Dale.

Dale, I loved can opener 3! I came to work on cloud nine, but I'm getting a little discouraged by some of my coworkers who are being negative.

The instant message pops up on Dale's computer, and he logs on.

Dale: *Bless your heart!*

Greg: *OK, I deserved that.*

Dale: *"For now we see through a glass, darkly; but then face to face: now I know in part; but then shall I know even as also I am known" (1 Corinthians 13:12).*

Greg: *One of my favorite scriptures. So how can I help the people at work get on the bandwagon?*

Dale: *First Corinthians 13:12 again. Can't help them, but I can help you see them better. We see only a little bit of people, the part they want us to see. You and I do the same thing to them. We like to show people the Greg and Dale we want them to see. This is because we aren't perfect. If we were perfect, we'd see them as they really are—hurting and in need. But since we aren't, we don't—we see them as, well, our problem, someone who is dragging us down, someone who reminds us that we aren't perfect either.*

Since we aren't perfect, let's pretend. We could pretend we are the only two people on the planet who can help everyone become better. Our job is to forgive and set an example. We aren't to judge, because if we judge we will have to fall under that same judgment. Not easy, is it?

Greg: *I see what you mean ... I should first try to be happy with myself. Then I'll be happy with others.*

Dale: *Good luck! I'm still working on me.*

Greg goes back to work and doesn't look for reasons to be upset. He avoids the traps of complaining and sets his mind on solving problems, being an optimist, and being happy. Something begins to happen. He gets his first affirmation when a coworker asks him if he's on a new diet or exercise program. When Greg asks why he thinks that, the man's answer is revolutionary: "You look great!"

Greg logs on to the computer when he gets home and sends the following message to Dale:

Others are happier, more optimistic, and better problem solvers when I work on me instead of them.

Dale: *BLESS YOUR HEART!*

CAN OPENER 4

MY BIG SURPRISE:

TRANSITION + REMISSION = TRANSMISSION
(THANKS, DAD!)

For whom the Lord loveth he correcteth; even as a father the son in whom he delighteth.—*PROVERBS 3:12.*

Our dads sometimes don't like us, but they always love us.
—*DALE HENRY, LOOSE TRANSLATION.*

Greg kicks back in his recliner. Yesterday was a barometer for him, a way to recognize the highs and lows of being an opener. He's starting to understand how his own behavior and inner thoughts control his performance and his expectations of others. He decides he will discard can'ts and begin replacing them with cans.

He thinks, *Monday has become such a dreaded day ... More people pass away on Monday than on any other day of the week ... I think I'm going to start looking forward to Monday—I'll make it my Independence Day.*

Greg reaches for a pen and pad and begins to write:

WHAT HAVE I LEARNED SO FAR?

- **Can Opener 1:** Openers find avenues where others find dead ends.

- **Can Opener 2:** Openers tell everyone their passion—shared excitement energizes the can.

- **Can Opener 3:** Openers understand that team members are happier, more optimistic, and better problem solvers when the opener is happy, optimistic, and a problem solver.

OK, Dale, what have you got for me today? Greg opens can 4 and begins to read.

Greg, we were both blessed with great dads, weren't we? My dad traveled with me a lot after he retired. (Looking back, I wish he'd been with me even more.) One of our adventures took us to Alaska, where I was to speak to a group of law-enforcement people. He loved it! He came away with two unique observations: It was the first time he didn't see the sun for three days, and he saw more snow in those three days than a Southern boy sees in a lifetime.

When the chief of police picked us up at the Anchorage airport, Dad kept going on about how he had never seen so much snow in one place. But it wasn't the snow that interested me. I've always had a secret desire for a moose head to hang on one of my walls in the den. So I asked the chief (nonchalantly) where someone might find a moose head for their wall. (I didn't want to shoot one—I was hoping I could find one that had died of natural causes.)

"I know just the place to go!" he said, and whipped the cruiser around in the middle of the street. A minute later we pulled up in front of a taxidermist's establishment. As soon as we walked in I knew I had hit pay dirt. There were moose heads everywhere!

"My friend here is looking for a moose head to take back home to Tennessee," the chief said to the proprietor. "Can you fix him up?"

Greg, there's a little place in Newport, Tennessee, that manufactures a substance that, well, let's just say it's a very high grade of alternative fuel. I personally have never bought any, of course, but they tell me that when you go there to make a purchase they "size you up."

When the chief asked for a moose head, this guy looked us up and down and said, "Fellows, it is illegal [a violation of federal law—you know, like manufacturing and distributing a very high grade of alternative fuel] to sell an Alaskan moose head that you have not shot yourself."

I tried unsuccessfully to wrap my mind around the fact that I was standing beside the chief of police of the city of Anchorage, Alaska, who had just broken several laws simply by asking for a moose head. So I thought I'd try to inject a little humor into the situation. "Do you have a head of a moose that died of old age?" I asked.

Taxidermist Man didn't crack a smile. "No way!" he said vehemently.

Interview over.

We were both pretty hungry after we got to the hotel, so we went into the restaurant for a bite. My dad is not into trying new things to eat. He's a biscuit-and-gravy-meat-and-potatoes-pinto-beans-and-corn-bread kind of guy, and his dietary preferences had gotten us in trouble a couple of times during our travels together.

One time in North Carolina he wanted to eat breakfast at a little greasy spoon off the beaten path. However, being well traveled, I don't trust any place that sells food that doesn't sport a score of at least a 90-plus from the health department, and I don't think the health department had ever found this place. Nevertheless, in we walked.

"This is what I'm talking about!" my dad said happily. "Finally! A restaurant that understands Southern cooking! I'll bet we can get some homemade biscuits and gravy and a great cup of coffee here."

I didn't share his enthusiasm on either count. As we sat down, a woman materialized from what looked like the kitchen at the back of the café. Her apron displayed a sampling of everything that had been on last week's menu. In her hands she carried a large lump of dough that she kneaded as she walked toward us. A dark substance trickled from the corner of her mouth from a dip she'd been nursing between her cheek and gum. "You boys want some biscuits and gravy?" she drawled. She was, as we say in the South, loaded up.

My dad swallowed hard and squeaked, "Nope. Just dry toast and coffee; that's all we ever eat for breakfast." (This from a man who hadn't begun a morning in his 70 years without biscuits and gravy for breakfast.) Two minutes later he was asking me how far it was to the interstate and the nearest Cracker Barrel.

On the other extreme of the culinary scale, we were in San Diego, California, one beautiful morning when I suggested a sidewalk café across from the bay. Dad began flipping the menu over and over, searching for his beloved biscuits and gravy, of course.

"What's wrong, Dad?" I asked.

"I can't find biscuits and gravy."

"This is California, Dad; they don't have biscuits and gravy."

He frowned. "I'm OK with that, son, but what in the world is a quiche" [Southern pronunciation: *quick-eeee]*"?

"That's fancy eggs, Dad, and I'm ordering."

Meanwhile, back in Alaska it's lunch, and he's hungry.

"Dad, how about some lentil-and-reindeer soup and some iced tea for a change?" I suggest.

"What's a lentil? And I'm not sure Santa would be too keen on the idea of us having Rudolph for lunch."

"We're in Alaska, Dad. What do you think? Let's give it a try! It can't be as bad as those biscuits and gravy in North Carolina, or the fancy eggs in California."

We laughed, and the meal was wonderful.

The next day I presented my programs. Afterward, some of the guys from the FBI recommended that we try a restaurant with a bit of local flair. I believe their exact words were "they have the best halibut in the city." When I'm somewhere different, I like to eat different. So I didn't ask Dad; I just said, "Let's go."

The agent took us to the coolest place I've ever seen. The restaurant featured a plane that looked as if it had crashed through the roof. And the food was the best—even Dad liked it. We hung around afterward and enjoyed the local entertainment before deciding it was time to go back to the hotel to rest up for the next day of meetings. I asked the waiter to call us a cab, and our next father–son adventure was under way.

Dad and I crawled into the back of the cab, an old 1980-ish Ford LTD land yacht, and gave the driver the name of our hotel. Now, this restaurant is positioned on the top of a mountain, a little detail that had escaped us, and the roads in Anchorage are totally invisible—everything is white. So you just kind of guess where you are and do your best to stay on them.

The farther down the hill we went, the more speed we picked up. I had no way of knowing what my dad was thinking, but I can assure you that he was as tense about this ride as I was, because we both knew that this particular downhill road ended at one of the major thoroughfares running through town.

We were gathering speed at a rather brisk rate, and Dad was getting taller and taller in his seat. At what must have been the appropriate time, the driver engaged the brakes. However, instead of slowing, that massive Ford began to pick up speed. Now both of us *and* the driver were getting a little tense. I tried to stay calm, thinking, *Hey, this guy has done this a thousand times.*

Twenty-five yards from the intersection our Ford missile hit a snowbank. Sliding from one side of the road to the other, we were caught up in some kind of pinball cab nightmare. I could see only the back of the driver's head, and it never wavered. Then five feet from the intersection friction, inertia, the snow, and the clenching of our rear ends in the back seat slowed us to a stop.

As we got out at the hotel I mentioned to the cab driver that we were from Tennessee. "That was a real piece of driving back there," I said. "You really had my dad and me going when you were coming off that snow- and ice-covered mountain! I'll bet you must have done that a hundred times, huh?"

It was then that I got my first good look at his face, which was so wet with sweat that it looked as if he'd just run a five-mile race. "I thought we were going to lose it back there in that turn," he quavered. "I just moved here last week, and tonight was my first night as a cab driver."

My dad digested this bit of information for a thoughtful moment, then said, "You did good, son. We're from the South. We love NASCAR, and if it isn't rubbin', it isn't racin'." Then my dad put his arm around my neck and said, "Let's get some shut-eye. I don't know how these folks up here know when it's time to go to bed, with it dark all the time."

As I crawled into bed and turned out the light I said, "Good night, Dad; I love you."

"Love you too, son; sleep well."

"Dad, can I ask you a question?"

"Sure, son; go ahead."

"Did it not scare you just a little when that cab driver started sliding around on that mountain?"

Dad began to snicker. "Son, if I had passed gas only a dog could have heard it."

Dad and I had many more adventures. I was able to take him as far as you could go to the north, south, east, and west in our beautiful country—and we saw tons of places in between. He was always there for me, showing me how harmless transitions are if you continue to live each day with joy. Greg, I realize now that my dad comprehended the real joy of remission—admitting your mistakes and transgressions, and asking forgiveness when forgiveness is needed. He was the transmission of our family, gearing up in good times and down in bad.

My dad is my hero. I will always love him. He is an opener.

Greg sits up in the recliner. *The opener uses the transmission of the can by working inside remission and transition … The opener must be willing to accept responsibility when things go wrong, and allow team members to make mistakes (seek forgiveness and give it).* Greg looks at his clock. *Wow! I've got to run.* He puts on his clothes and grabs his car keys, and he's off.

At work Greg is networking and listening to those around him. He gives feedback and positive affirmation about possible outcomes to challenges his work group is trying to meet. At 10:30 he's called on to be an opener: an associate has let an important time line slip, and everyone goes into blame mode. Greg knows that he must be a transmission. He calls a meeting, and resources are realigned as everyone pitches in. The deadline is missed only marginally. What could have been a disaster, with everyone playing the blame game, now has had an alternative ending. The project is a success (transition + remission = transmission); everyone has moved forward.

Home once more, Greg has dinner, then logs on and types: *The opener uses work transitions by shifting resources, not blame. I think I am starting to get the hang of this!*

CAN OPENER 5

PREPARING FOR THE GREATEST ENEMY: THE LID

I can of mine own self do nothing: as I hear, I judge: and my judgment is just; because I seek not mine own will, but the will of the Father which hath sent me. —*JOHN 5:30.*

Seek God and His will, and your container will be filled.
—*DALE HENRY, LOOSE TRANSLATION.*

It's the middle of the week! Greg is now in the groove. He decides to get ready for work and go out for some breakfast. (All that talk in can 4 about biscuits and gravy must have awakened his appetite psyche.) He opens can 5, unrolls its contents, and sticks it in his pocket. At the restaurant he orders breakfast and begins to read.

Greg, every opener is going to have to face the lid. The opener cannot help the lid. Unlike the can, the lid is screwed on—an opener is the wrong tool for the wrong job. The lid has caused the downfall of many openers because the lid knows our weaknesses.

George was a successful businessman. He was doing all the right things, speaking to all the right people, making all the right investments. He was an opener. Like many successful people, he understood that happiness is more likely to bring you success than success is to bring you happiness. George had a great wife, family, and social life. You could say that he had the best of everything. Comfortable and content, George was at the top of his game.

Any successful person will tell you that affluence is a lid. You begin to think you are a pretty smart dude, like the rich young man who asked Jesus what else he needed to do to inherit eternal life. We sometimes ask questions, but we don't want answers—we want affirmations. Success causes us to listen to our own advice (much like lawyers who represent themselves), and the lid is in place.

George didn't really do anything wrong. He didn't break the law, steal, or commit a crime—*he just stopped opening cans.* It started out pretty innocently. A couple of changes and some mistakes during transitions, and the cycle repeated itself until it looked as though everything was going wrong. Everything wasn't really going wrong—that was just how George saw it. He began changing his behavior, little things at first, and then he became hard to deal with.

The lid divides the house against itself. Everything from business relationships to his family life began, in George's mind, to fall apart. The truth was, George just stopped being George. His health and self-confidence became a downward spiraling, self-fulfilling nightmare. He made appointments with doctors and specialists who could offer him no cure for the ailment that he seemed to have contracted.

Finally he found a doctor who gave him the escape he thought he needed: pills for sleep, pills for energy, and pills for anxiety. He was on the brink of losing it all. He turned to a friend who recommended a Christian counselor. *I don't need counseling—I need help,* George thought.   Nevertheless, he gave in and made an appointment.

At first George felt a little uncomfortable sharing intimate details of his life with a total stranger, but after the first hour he began to feel better just to get a few problems off his chest. Then the counselor said, "George, I want to give you a little something that will help you get your life back into perspective again."

Oh, great, George thought. *Another prescription—just what I need.*

The counselor handed him four small envelopes numbered from 1 to 4. "George, I want you to take tomorrow off."

"I can't do that!" George yelled. "Haven't you been listening? My life is in ruins. I can't leave those people at the office unsupervised! All they need is another excuse to put me into bankruptcy."

"I understand your need to be there, George, but if I'm going to help you, you must trust me," the counselor said.

George looked at his hands, knotted in his lap. "OK," he said finally. "When do you want me to start taking these pills?"

"First, George, let's talk about tomorrow." The counselor asked him if he'd had a special place he'd liked to visit when he was a little boy.

"I enjoyed fishing," George told him.

The counselor took each of the four envelopes and wrote times on them. "George, I want you to go to the white-water stream on the other side of town. Get there about 8:00 in the morning. There's a bend in the stream, right off Willow Park Road. Do you know it?"

"Yes, I know where that is."

"Good. Go there and sit near the sandbar. Have a good breakfast and pack a lunch; you're going to be there awhile. And go alone—this day is just for you, George. Tell no one where you are going, leave your cell phone at home, and record a nice message on your voice mail. Do you have any questions?"

"Yes. What am I going to do all day at the stream that I can't do at my office? I'm an important man—I don't have time to go off lollygagging next to some creek. And what about my medication? I'll need my medication!"

"I'm sure your medication is important," the counselor calmly explained, "but please leave it at home."

This made George even more anxious. He wasn't sure that this guy wasn't some sort of nut. But even though he was a little uncomfortable, he did as he was asked. He got up early and had a big breakfast. He packed a large lunch and arrived at the river around 8:00, as he was instructed. He sat down by the sand-bar and pulled the four small envelopes from his pocket and noticed that each envelope had a time written on the front: one envelope was to be opened at 8:00, the next at 10:00, the third at noon, and the last one at 2:00.

George tore open the 8:00 envelope and pulled out a folded piece of paper. The note said: MAKE YOURSELF COMFORTABLE. CLOSE YOUR EYES AND THINK OF WHERE YOU ARE.

George was furious! "I am out here in the middle of nowhere on a creek bank," he fumed, "and my counselor wants me to daydream."

After a couple minutes he decided that nothing else had seemed to help, so he might as well give it a try. First, he relaxed. Then he made himself comfortable on the blanket that he'd brought with his lunch. Closing his eyes, he began to think about where he was . . .

It was peaceful and quiet.

The only sound he could hear was the water gently gurgling over the rocks in the stream . . . Then he began to hear the birds' sweet music, first from the left, then from the right. They seemed to be everywhere!

He could smell the sweet grass and the autumn leaves. He recognized the unforgettable aroma of the musty, wet earth near the edge of the stream.

The sun was warm—it was the most comfortable he had been in some time. As he lay there, just at the edge of sleep, he rolled over and looked at his watch. It was 10:00.

The note in the second envelope instructed: LIE BACK AND RELAX AND REMEMBER THE BLESSINGS OF LIFE.

At first, all he could think about were his troubles. Then, slowly, he began to relax as he remembered his wife and their courtship ... How happy they had been when they first met and were married!

He remembered the birth of his children and all the joy they had brought him ...

Then there were his friends who had helped him get started in business ...

He began to think about how his family had worshipped together, and all the support the church had been to them in those early years ...

Friends, associates, customers—practically everyone in town played through his mind like a movie at a drive-in theater. He began to understand how tremendously blessed his life had truly been. Time seemed to fold in on itself as he floated from the past to the present, and then to the past again and back.

Then it was 12:00. Where had the day gone? Opening the third small envelope, he immediately unfolded the paper he found inside and read it aloud: "WHERE CAN GOD TAKE YOU FROM HERE?"

It had been easy to comply with the instructions on the other notes. George knew this request was going to require something totally different, a commitment. He had forgotten God. In the busyness of life he had pushed God out.

Man is nothing without God.

George is nothing without God.

George thought he had become God.

Greg, we're all like George. Success is important, and we should celebrate our success and the success of others. Too often, though, success becomes a lid that closes us inside ourselves.

George changed his position on the blanket; he went from restful to restless. He felt helpless and small. His world was beginning to close in, and right before it crashed—George decided to give it to God.

Openers need to be opened. There is no such thing as a stand-alone leader. George had stopped being an opener and had settled for being—a lid.

It was the most excruciating—and freeing—two hours of his life. Giving over everything to God is the supreme sacrifice. The rich man had walked right up to it—and walked away (Mark 10:22).

George was changed.

It was 2:00, and he ripped open the last envelope. The note read: LOOK FOR THE RED FLAG, AND DIG UP YOUR FUTURE.

Do what? *What red flag?* George turned around. Behind him, in the sand, was a small red flag. *It must have been left there by a child,* he thought. When he pulled it up, though, he could see that something was buried underneath. Digging with his fingers, he finally pulled out a small glass jar. "Open it, if you can" was written on the lid.

The lid was screwed on tight, and George struggled hard to remove it. Inside was another note and a photo of the world with George's name in the center. Above the world his counselor had written: *George, do you see anything wrong with this picture?* And suddenly George got it. He was *not* the center of the world—God needed to be the center.

He gathered up his belongings. He had conquered the lid.

Greg, even good Christians have lids. None of us are perfect—far from it! My grandfather used to say that none of us will live long enough to make all the mistakes we could make.

We all fail.

Openers fail. But openers know where to go when they fail: to the feet of the Master.

A vessel is only as good as its contents. The opener is first filled; then he can help others to be filled.

Greg folds up the story from the fifth can and puts it into his pocket. He slowly finishes his meal and leaves a tip. Things are clicking in his head as he thinks about the lid. He's still reflecting about what he'd read as he pays for his breakfast and drives to work. His work performance had been suffering because of his attitude. It's that red flag—the future—that's bothering him.

Alone in his office, he says what is in his heart: "Maybe the red flag isn't my job. Maybe the red flag is me."

He begins to go through old files of work projects that he had started but never finished. These projects from the past had seemed unimportant and demeaning to him, busywork handed down from a supervisor who didn't have the time to deal with them. Now new ideas begin to flow through his open work attitude. He isn't in the center anymore; he is removing old work lids that he'd been putting on for years.

After work Greg sends Dale his thoughts on can 5:

Dale, the opener can do nothing without divine intervention. The lid flourishes when we put ourselves in the center of our world. The opener recognizes the red flag of transition and moves through everyday tasks to regain value. The vessel is cleansed only when the lid of self-doubt is destroyed.

Greg realizes how much he's grown during the past five days. His confidence, work ethic, team spirit, and faith have been restored to new levels. He calls his mother and tells her about the cans. He calls his son, and they plan an outing together for the weekend. He's going to the gym, working out and feeling good. He's meditating and seeking wisdom as he sorts through years of baggage and self-imposed mediocrity. He's beginning to look at and to respond to life like an opener.

CAN OPENER 6

THE GREATEST REVIVAL:

HOW TO GET YOUR TEAM'S "WHACK" BACK

Be glad in the Lord, and rejoice, ye righteous: and shout for joy, all ye that are upright in heart. —*PSALM 32:11.*

The only way to get your whack back is through joy.
—*DALE HENRY, LOOSE TRANSLATION.*

The next morning is rainy and muggy. Greg pulls the curtain back in his living room, then moves to the kitchen. A staff meeting is scheduled for today. *OK, Dale,* he mutters to himself, *I need something special today. Hit me with your best shot. I need a can-do can!* He pries the lid off can 6 and reads the following story:

Last summer I went with my kids on spring break—they asked me to go! (How cool is that?) At Orlando's Universal Studios an artist did a character portrait of LeAnne, Keith (LeAnne's fiancé), Lauren, and Brandon (Lauren's fiancé). As I watched him draw their exaggerated features, I was pleasantly surprised at how well he had captured the essences of the quartet. LeAnne's beautiful, elongated face; Keith's crooked, turned-up smile; Lauren's lovely large eyes; and Brandon's animated eyebrows—all were right on target. The artist had expressed their "whack."

What is whack, you ask? Whack is our personality, our joy; it is what makes us, well, unique. My whack happens to be speaking and observing the human element. Keith, the chemist (my future son-in-law), would argue that there is no such thing as the human element, because it isn't on the periodic table. (Well, I think they should add it, because the human element reacts with everything. This reaction and interaction is what makes us interesting!)

Let me give you another example. Michelle, my office manager, does the majority of the day-to-day operations in our office. She receives the phone calls, keeps the calendar, and manages the accounts payable and accounts receivable. Simply put, she does all the work; I have all the fun. I rarely get a phone call at home about a speaking event until Michelle has checked the calendar. So when someone calls me, it's always about what topic they'd like me to speak on, not when I'm to appear.

One day I was catching up on some e-mails in my office when my phone rang. "Good afternoon, Dr. Dale," the voice on the other end of the line said. "Jimmy Goodman here."

(I knew from his greeting that he'd just gotten off the phone with Michelle. When someone calls me Dr. Dale, it's because Michelle calls me Dr. Dale.) He said that he had heard me speak in St. Louis at an insurance convention, and he would love to have me present at their upcoming conference in Las Vegas.

Because of the arrangement we have in my office (I don't book, and Michelle doesn't speak), I was a little confused as to why this man was talking to me about a speaking date. Before I could ask, he said, "Like I said, I'd love to have you come and present for us—but you can't."

I said that I was sorry—that sometimes my calendar fills up quickly.

He interrupted. "No, Dr. Dale, you're not speaking that day—you just can't do our convention."

In situations like this I begin to talk to myself. *Well, if I'm not speaking somewhere else, why can't I do this man's meeting?*

"You can't present for us because our meeting is on October 23," he explained.

Now it all made sense! That's our anniversary! For obvious reasons, I don't travel or present on our anniversary.

"Do you and your wife ever travel on your anniversary, Dr. Dale?"

"Sometimes we like to travel," I said cautiously.

"Have you ever gone to Las Vegas on your anniversary?"

I knew where this was going.

"We'd love to have you speak at our convention," he invited, "and then you and your wife could stay on as our guests at the convention."

"Well," I said, "I'll have to think about that." (Which is man talk for "I'll have to ask my wife.")

He said that he'd love to get us a very nice suite for the weekend, and that they'd take care of us as honored guests.

Sounded like a pretty sweet deal to me, so I headed down to the kitchen and grabbed an apple off the counter. "Hey, Deb," I said casually, "how would you like to go to Las Vegas for our anniversary?"

"So, someone wants you to speak there, right?" Deb is quick on the uptake. She had me.

"Well, what do you think, honey? It's just a keynote, and the rest of the three days would be all ours to see shows, shop, and eat."

She shrugged. "Why not?"

So I called Mr. Goodman back and said, "I've decided that your idea is great!" (Which is man talk for "my wife said I could come.") We discussed topics, and Michelle took care of the rest.

Debra doesn't travel well. She hates the hassle of airports and security because she always gets screened for security, and her luggage gets rifled. Somehow my wife must look like a terrorist. Forget the old adage about a woman scorned—nothing's worse than a woman *searched.*

On our way to the airport that morning Deb asked, "How do you do it, honey?"

"How do I do what?"

"How do you travel without losing your temper? It seems as though every time we go somewhere I get checked by security. Don't you hate it when people go through your things? How can you stay calm while a complete stranger goes through your luggage and touches all your private things?"

I laughed. "Hey, to me it's funny. I get even. After I've been on the road a couple days I take my dirty underwear and put it on top in my suitcase. You should see their faces!"

"Come on, honey; don't you hate taking your shoes off and walking on that dirty floor?"

"Do you know why we have to do that?"

"I know that I don't like it."

"Deb, a couple years ago some nut tried to get on a plane with a bomb in his shoe. I'm glad he didn't put it in his underwear—which would you rather take off?"

We both laughed, and it seemed to help take the anxiousness out of the moment. I began praying constantly that this trip would be uneventful. We got on the plane at Knoxville without a hitch. No security issues, the flight was on time, and we got great seats together with plenty of legroom. As we were getting comfortable, a woman who was traveling with her nine (yes, I said nine) children got on board.

"Look how well behaved they are!" Debra whispered.

I was thinking that her husband needed to get a hobby. But Debra was right—these stair-step siblings were very well behaved. As the older children helped care for the younger children, we looked at each other and said at almost the same time, "Military kids!"

We were right—they were going back after a visit home. The youngest child was enjoying a large chocolate sucker. It looked mighty tasty—and mighty sticky. At first the children were able to keep the damage from the messy, chocolate-covered infant to a minimum. But in the span of about 10 minutes the chocolate went from her hands to all over her small body. She even had chocolate on the soles of her feet.

"She is so cute!" Deb cooed to the baby's mother.

Mothers can look right through the mess and see a child (that's a mother's "whack"). I was thinking that she was going to have to hose her daughter down to get all that chocolate off of her and her clothes. But the baby didn't seem to mind, her brothers and sisters didn't seem to mind, her mother didn't seem to mind, and Debra and I were setting far enough away so that we didn't mind.

Our young flight attendant took one look at this little girl and said, "You are a messy miss." Sizing up the child and the chocolate sucker, she asked, "Do you want some help, ma'am, cleaning her up?"

The mother just smiled and said, "No, honey, it would probably be easier to have another one than to clean this one up."

We all laughed.

We changed planes in Atlanta and began our second leg to Las Vegas. It was wonderful—the weather was great, and the flight was smooth. When we got to Vegas, we didn't have to wait for a cab, there was no line anywhere, and we went straight to the hotel. I thought I was home free—a day of problem-free travel is a beautiful thing!

We walked into the lobby and up to the counter. "Hi!" I greeted the clerk. "My name is Dale Henry, and my wife and I have a reservation."

She turned to the computer and entered my name. She studied the screen a moment; then a funny but worried look crossed her face, and she said, "H'm-mmmm. Well, *huh!*"

I waited for the next sentence, which I was sure was not going to be "You just won the lottery!" Instead, she smiled a polite smile and said, "I need to get the manager."

Now, I travel more than 180 times a year, and my experience has taught me that this could mean only trouble for the Henry family. Deb stepped closer to me, sensing that something was not going right.

Soon the manager came out of his office and studied the monitor. "H'mm-mmm. Well, *huh!*" (Obviously both he and the clerk had been to the same communications workshop.) Then the manager looked at us and said, "Dr. Henry, we have a little problem."

My experience has been that when a hotel manager says he has a problem, it means that *I* have a problem.

"Dr. Henry," he continued, "your client—and our customer—reserved one of our nicest suites for you and your wife. Unfortunately, we had a high roller who came into town a couple days ago and lost a significant amount of money in our casino. He's in your room. I would like him to stay there. But that presents a problem since we promised both you and him the same room. So here's what we're going to do. I understand you and your wife are celebrating your anniversary, and I want to make sure it's one you remember for years. We're going to give you our honeymoon suite and some show tickets. I would also like to treat you to dinner at any of our restaurants while you are here. Would that be satisfactory to you and your wife, Dr. Henry?"

"Y-e-s," I stammered. "Thank you! That would be great!"

We took our key and made our way to the honeymoon suite. As we opened the door, we saw … mirrors! There were mirrors everywhere—on the walls, on the ceiling; there were even mirrored tiles on the bathroom floor. I am 52 years old, and the last thing I need is mirrors providing a visual perspective at every turn. And the bed! It was a heart-shaped thing that your legs hang off of, no matter which way you try to arrange yourself.

The next morning I gave my presentation, and we had a blast. By the time I got back to the room Deb had left for a little shopping, so I lay down on one of those French couches (you know, the kind with only one arm). The hotel must get a real deal on these things because they buy them in bulk. I fell asleep, and sometime during my nap Deb got back from shopping. She slipped into the bathroom and took a shower (you know how exhausting shopping can be).

When she stepped out of the shower, I was still sleeping. I must be a funny sleeper, because my family is always taking pictures of me sleeping. We have hundreds of pictures of me drooling and snoozing. Deb picked up the camera and squeezed off several more snapshots for their collection.

The hotel people were as good as their word—it was an anniversary we will never forget. The trip back was uneventful, and my travel itinerary continued. After two days on the road I was home again, eating breakfast, when Deb said, "I have the pictures from our anniversary trip." (Let me translate that in man talk: Deb is going to look at the pictures, and if she likes them, I will get to see them too.)

It's like a Saturday travelogue. Picking up the pictures, she begins, "Oh, here we are packing the car . . . This is a great shot of you taking out our luggage at the airport . . . I *love* this picture—I got that sweet young mother and her family, the one with the little chocolate-covered girl . . . Here are some shots out the plane window . . . I got a picture of the hotel manager; he was so nice!"

Suddenly her facial features changed, registering severe shock. "Oh, my *goodness!* Dale, there are pictures here of me in my *underwear!*"

The mirrors! She hadn't taken them into account when she was so happily taking pictures of me snoozing. I know; I should have kept this to myself, but you should have seen the look on Deb's face when I said that I bet the boys at the Wal-Mart photo lab had fun developing those shots.

The expressions on *our* faces, Greg, are our whack. Retailers will tell you that the *outside* of the can is more important than the *inside*. The opener makes sure the outside (our face) is doing its job by showing joy during transition.

Greg smiles. He thinks, *I just got whacked! Today's staff meeting is going to be different.* And thanks to Greg, no one got out of whack. Later, setting his gym bag down in the living room, he makes his way to the computer and sends the following e-mail to Dale:

Dale, the opener should never get out of whack. Instead, he puts people back in whack by opening cans. Thanks!

Your brother, Greg

WHAT HAVE I LEARNED SO FAR?

- **Can Opener 4:** Openers use the transmission of the can by working inside remission and transition.

- **Can Opener 5:** The vessel is cleansed only when the lid of self-doubt is destroyed.

- **Can Opener 6:** Openers should never get out of whack. Instead, they put people back in whack by opening cans.

CAN OPENER

7

THE GIFT OF INTEGRITY:

MOM WAS RIGHT—"IF IT'S EASY TO SAY, KEEP IT TO YOURSELF."

If any man think that he knoweth any thing, he knoweth nothing yet as he ought to know.—*1 CORINTHIANS 8:2.*

Most of us just ain't that smart, but if we keep our mouth shut no one will know.—*DALE HENRY, LOOSE TRANSLATION.*

Greg is excited as he dresses. There's a leadership training workshop off-site today. He grabs can 7 and opens it at the breakfast table and begins to read its contents.

Technology has gotten a little out of hand. From time to time I find myself talking to someone at the airport and suddenly realize they aren't talking to me. In their ear they have a Bluetooth, a small device that enables them to have hands-free communication from their cell phone. And there I am, having a nice conversation with someone who is having a nice conversation—with someone else. How embarrassing is that? Shouldn't technology make our lives easier? Let me give you some examples of technology run amok.

Go to any public bathroom and try to get soap without wiggling your hand under the soap dispenser. I'm a simple kind of guy, and I like to *pump* my own soap. Technologically savvy soap dispensers tend to put the soap wherever my hand *isn't*. And when I want water, I have to wiggle my hand to set off the motion detector that provides water for washing.

Several weeks ago I was in a Birmingham, Alabama, restroom, trying to wash my hands. There I stood, flailing my hands back and forth, trying to get water from the faucet, when the guy next to me leans over and says, "There's a handle right there, mister." I felt like a goober.

The technology gurus didn't stop with the water and soap. Now you have to wave to get a paper towel from its dispenser. And if there's a single inch of towel sticking out, forget waving—you're not getting another inch until you rip that first inch off.

Let's not get started on the automatic commode flushers other than saying it bothers me a great deal to still be enthroned when the commode decides it needs to do an automatic courtesy flush without consulting me first. *This is better?* They have crossed the line! Let me elaborate.

I am in Chicago, Illinois, minding my own business. On the commode in front of me is a device that I can describe only as a thing that looks like a shower cap that's stretched around the perimeter of the seat. On the wall is a button that once engaged sends a fresh lid covering snaking around the seat. The covering comes out of the wall on the right, slides around the commode seat, and retreats back into the wall on the left.

I pondered on this for some time. You see, I come from a reference point in the past that after you washed your hands you'd reach up and pull down on a cloth towel dispenser (a *real* cloth dispenser). Everyone knew that it was the same cloth towel—it just went round and round in a continuous circle. So here I stand in Chicago, looking at this commode, and I think, *I'll bet that seat cover goes around my commode, through the wall, and then around the commode on the other side. All we are doing is swapping this thing all day long!* So I pull out my pen, put a mark on the seat cover, and push the button.

Around it goes.

I mark on it again, and again push the button.

From the stall next door a fellow with a Southern accent says, "It's not the same one. I checked it last week."

Ever notice how good it makes you feel to get things like this—things that are bothering you—out? It is so freeing just to bare your heart and mind. Well, sort of, although silence is sometimes not only golden, it is downright priceless.

After five days on the road I was going to Gulfport, Mississippi, to speak to a large technology company on the topic of integrity. I had gotten a recommendation from their VP of IT (vice president of information technology for my less-technological friends, bless your heart), and I was going to be speaking right after the CEO's presentation.

I was tired. I understand the system. You don't make it to million-mile status on an airline without understanding the system. When you fly Delta, you are put into categories, depending on how frequently you fly: silver at the low end; then gold; and finally platinum for the most frequent fliers. I'm aluminum, the category for those of us who live on planes.

Flying from Cincinnati, I was to change planes in Atlanta, then fly on down to Gulfport. (I know—Cincinnati and Atlanta are both hubs. Don't get me started.) Arriving at the gate in Cincinnati, I positioned myself. (Remember? I know the system.) Frequent flyers are allowed to board first, and I was ready to get on and take a nap. Like a runner in a starting block I was primed. When the flight was called to board, I was first in line. I wanted to get on the plane, put my feet up on my carry-on bag, and go to sleep. I made it outside and put my roller bag on the planeside check-in cart. While I was loading my bag, the guy behind me shot into the line ahead of me. I know there's not an actual rule about passing someone in line, but come on!

Too late. He was on the stairs and into the plane. Of all the people on the planet to get in front of me, it would have to be someone who didn't understand flying physics. An extremely large bag will not go into an extremely small overhead bin. But that didn't keep him from trying. He blocked the aisle while he pushed and pushed, but the bag wouldn't budge. Every 10 seconds he would turn to me and say, "As quick as I get can this bag into the overhead I'll get out of your way."

It's healthy to talk to yourself. What is not healthy is to say something that's easy to say. You know what I mean—something that rolls off the tongue and feels so good to say. You need to keep that to yourself! But oh, how I wanted to say, "Well, let me just call Social Security for a change of address, because we're going to be here awhile, and I don't want to miss my first check, which is due to arrive in about 15 years." I could have said that, but what would have been the outcome?

At one time I was a Rotarian. Would my response have met the Rotary "four-way test":

Is it the truth?

Is it fair to all concerned?

Will it build goodwill and better friendships?

Will it be beneficial to all concerned?

No, no, no, and no.

Oh, there were plenty of people behind me who wanted to tell this man where he could put his bag. Several people in that long line were giving advice out loud that, well, let's just say wasn't helpful.

After several eternal minutes I looked at this fellow and asked, "You fly much?"

Still struggling with his bag, he grunted, "Way too much. Mostly overseas travel for business. You know, long flights and bad food."

"You fly on CRJs much?"

He stopped and looked at me. "What's a CRJ?"

"Canadair Regional Jets—small commuter jets like this one."

"No," he said.

"I didn't think so," I said. "I bet that bag is pretty important."

"Yes, it is," he puffed. "I have a presentation tomorrow, and I need to work on it."

"Can I give you a recommendation? Why don't you take out your computer and your work, and let me take that bag down to the planeside check-in for you?"

"Oh, I don't think that will work. I have a close connection in Atlanta, and I don't have time to go to baggage claim."

"They'll give it back to you planeside in Atlanta when we land," I assured him.

"Hey, thanks! I didn't know the system." He got out his computer and paperwork and handed me the bag. I began walking through this sea of unhappy people (who, by the way, thought I was the one who had been holding up the flight).

I got on the plane last. I had a wonderful nap. I got off the plane in Atlanta, and rushed to catch my plane going to Gulfport. I read the *USA Today* on the short flight to the coast, and got off the plane and jumped in my rental car to drive to the Beau Rivage Hotel and check in.

The next morning I walked to the main ballroom to do my presentation. In the grand hall was the president whose presentation I was to follow. You guessed it—it was my friend from the commuter plane.

This could have turned out differently had I said something that was the least bit sarcastic. I was at this seminar to speak on integrity. My integrity stayed in check because my mouth stayed shut. No matter how good the lesson, there is always a caveat. I like the advice of President Eisenhower. Before he was president he formulated a way to deal with statements that were spoken out of anger. He would write a letter to the person who had angered him and put it in his desk drawer. If he still thought it was important a week later, he would send it. Reflection and a tempering of our responses is important to our integrity. It keeps our pride in check.

A month ago I received a wonderful call from a gentleman who had heard me speak in Baltimore, Maryland. He had called Michelle to reserve a speaking date, then immediately called me.

"Dr. Henry, we are so pleased that you are coming to our symposium. Your humor and insight will add to the meeting."

You can imagine how delighted I was to hear from someone who was so excited about me speaking to their organization!

"The symposium at the Harvard Graduate School of Business has a long-standing tradition of inviting authors and speakers who will add to the ever-widening body of knowledge of our attendees," he continued.

I was absolutely as giddy as a schoolgirl that I was going to speak at Harvard! This was like Tiger Woods calling and asking if I wanted to tee up on the front nines at Sawgrass. As Barney Fife would say, "Andy, this is big—this is *real* big." I wanted to tell everyone. Every conversation I had I would somehow wiggle in the fact that I would be speaking at Harvard. Most of the time folks would say "That's nice" (read "bless your heart"). The problem is, what's important to you isn't always to everyone else.

The weeks passed, but my excitement didn't dampen in the least. Finally I was leaving for Boston, where I was going to speak at Harvard! When I arrived at the airport, the nice ladies from Delta asked, "Where are you off to today, Dr. Dale?"

I smiled nonchalantly and said, "Oh, I'm speaking at Harvard tomorrow."

They all *oohed* and *ahhed* and exclaimed, "Wow! That's great!"

It was wonderful. I got on the plane and landed in Atlanta. The word about where I was going must have traveled quickly, because they upgraded me to first class for my flight to Boston.

My seatmate leaned over and said, "So where are you off to today, sir?"

(Now, anyone who travels has probably had the passenger seated next to them say, "So, you going to Boston [or wherever]?" Being a humorist, I have to grab my tongue. It would be so easy to grin and say, "No, I'm going to jump out of the plane around Washington, D.C.")

Smiling broadly, I answered, "I'm going to Boston! I'm speaking for the Harvard Graduate School of Business tomorrow." I knew it was more information than he wanted, but I just loved saying it one more time.

Smiling even more broadly, he said, "The symposium that's starting tomorrow?"

"Yes, that's the one!"

"I'm attending that conference as well. Did you graduate from Harvard?" he asked, a little "note" in his voice.

"No," I said. "I have my bachelor's and master's degrees from the University of Tennessee and my doctorate from the University of Southern Mississippi."

Looking decidedly unimpressed, he nodded his head. "Oooh . . . I see."

Undeterred, I asked, "So, I guess you went to Harvard?"

"Yes indeed! Class of 1976."

It was plain to see that this man was so proud that he had attended Harvard. And I was proud for him—but that was no excuse for him to pooh-pooh *my* degrees. Have you ever had someone say something to you, and then a couple of hours later you think, *Now, here is what I* wish *I had answered*? Yeah; we've all done that. And I had a couple hours to sit on that plane and ponder. ("Pondering" is what Southern people do when we want to think something through.) Then, near the end of the flight, I leaned back over on the console between us and asked, "So you went to Harvard, and I guess you paid to go there, right?"

He smiled expansively. "Yes indeed!"

I carefully leaned back in my seat. "Well," I said, "they're paying me to come."

We both laughed.

Openers know when to hold their tongue and when to exercise it to bring things into perspective. When something should be said, it is our responsibility to speak up and clarify. A common misconception is that meek means weak. Meek means to speak and act with wisdom and integrity.

Greg shakes his head and laughs and remembers the many times he wished he'd held his tongue when words came so easy. Grabbing his car keys, he slides into his car and heads off to the retreat.

The leadership training is very timely, and his ears and mind are alert to new opportunities and new ideas. When he gets home, he e-mails Dale:

The opener uses discretion—speaking and listening, communicating and disseminating. By using this can, the opener gains wisdom and integrity.

CAN OPENER

THE GIFT OF VALUE: WHAT IS IT WORTH?

A gift is as a precious stone in the eyes of him that hath it: whithersoever it turneth, it prospereth.—*PROVERBS 17:8.*

Value is in our heart—giving it to others makes it more precious to us.—*DALE HENRY, LOOSE TRANSLATION.*

Greg rolls out of bed at 9:30 the next morning. He thinks, *Wow, I can't remember the last time I slept in this late. It sure feels wonderful!* He showers and slips on his shorts and golf shirt. He wants this day to be special—he and his son plan to spend the day together, playing golf and hanging out. The last thing he wants is for the past to get in the way of their future relationship.

After loading his golf clubs and shoes into his bag, he goes to the kitchen and opens can 8.

Greg, I have great clients! Presenting to a chamber of commerce group is always a treat because the majority of their members are small business owners.

I was working in Pigeon Forge, Tennessee, this past summer, doing a series of workshops on customer service. You know that I love to hug people. I get a charge out of telling people that appreciation is the most valuable thing we do for our employees, customers, family, and friends. There has to be a million ways to show people we care for them, but I prefer the hug.

During one of the presentations I picked the biggest guy in the room and said, "I'm a hugger." He immediately jumped to his feet and gave me a big bear hug. It was great!

Later that day the meeting coordinator came up to me, put his arm around my shoulder, and asked me a very unusual question: "Dr. Henry, what can I do *just* for you?"

On the surface this doesn't look or sound that different. All of us have had someone say Can I help you? or Can I do something for you? But he asked me what he could do *just* for me. Now, that's different. He didn't ask if there was something he could do for my family. He wanted to take care of something I wanted personally. There's no way to answer that question without being self-ish. I said, "Ted, I don't believe anyone has ever asked me that before. I will, however, take you up on your hospitality, because there is something you can do *just* for me. I'm a big fan of one of your local businesspeople, and it's been a couple of years since I've had the opportunity to say hi. So if you want to do something *just* for me, I'd love to just say hi to Ms. Dolly Parton."

He laughed. "Dr. Dale, you are never going to believe this, but several folks who were in your training sessions today would like for you to have lunch with them—and Dolly is going to be there."

So we went to the lunch, and I sat at the table with Dolly.

You know, I'm possibly the most blessed man you will ever meet. I was born into what I believe to be the best family on the planet. I talk to my mom and dad every day, whether I'm at home or away, and our conversation always ends with the same four words: "I love you, son."

I have two beautiful daughters, and no matter where I am in the world we always talk to each other, and our conversation always ends with the same four words: "I love you, Dad."

My wife, the love of my life, always ends our discussions with the same four words: "I love you, honey."

So there I sat, Greg, with Dolly Parton, and she looked at me and said four words that if I live to be 150 I will never forget: "I'm a hugger too!"

I said, "Let's get to it!"

We all laughed. What an amazingly genuine and remarkable person. The great lesson here—

Pay attention, Greg—forget the hug; we're moving on now.

The great lesson here is that all of us want to be appreciated. We never tire of people telling us we have value. But what is value, exactly? It really depends on the person you ask.

If you ask the ladies in my family, they'll say, "Where's the sale?" They can buy two of everything. Quantity.

If you ask my dad and me, we'll say, "It's on sale—but how long will it last?" Quality.

Men and women are sometimes very different. When the men in my family go shopping, we just want to get it over with. Most of the women in my life don't want it to ever end.

Have you ever eaten out with just men, Greg? When you're sitting in a restaurant with only men, there are two questions you will never hear:

"Greg, do you see that big guy in the buffet line? Is my butt as big as his butt?" This is not going to happen.

"Greg, I'm going to the men's room—you want to go?" And *that* is definitely not happening.

I've got this down to a fine science. There can be 500 people in an audience—250 men, and 250 women. I can say, "Why don't we take a 10-minute bathroom break." Every man in the room will be back in their seats in 10 minutes. And all the women will still be in line.

Do you know why? While women are in the ladies' room, they have meaningful conversations about everything from dresses, to office politics, to children, to what they thought of the speaker. They even have furniture in there (this is hearsay, of course—I've never been in the ladies' room). Men, on the other hand, don't talk, don't look at each other, and don't acknowledge each other's existence while in the men's room.

One morning Debra and I were having breakfast at Cracker Barrel (good biscuits and gravy) when she excused herself to go to the restroom. I told her I'd wait to order till she got back. And I did. Five minutes . . . 10 minutes . . . Finally, 15 minutes later, she came back and sat down. I could have *built* a bathroom in that time!

"Where have you been, honey?" I asked.

"I was in the ladies' room."

Smiling sweetly, I said, "What could you have possibly done in the ladies' room that could have taken 15 minutes?"

"Oh," she said, "there was a lady in the stall next to mine who had on the loveliest pair of emerald-green shoes, and we were talking about her shoes."

Sorry, Greg. I cannot imagine sitting in the men's room, looking under the divider at some old boy's britches down around his ankles and inquiring about his work boots.

But we all see value differently. We all see things from the inside out. Try this exercise: Roll your eyes back in your head and take a good look at your brain . . .

Oh. You can't do that?

OK. Bite your own teeth . . .

Yeah; you can't do that, either.

How about this—try tickling yourself . . . (On second thought, don't try that, either. Trust me—you can't do it.)

The only way you can see your own face is to use a reflective device. That's why our reality is our own—it is unique to us. Openers who learn from this exercise grasp the value of everyone's perspective because it belongs to them and them alone.

So what is value? Most of us think in terms of money. If something costs $10, then it's worth $10, right? Nope. Don't think so! Have you been shopping lately? The next time you buy something, pay attention to the transition of value in service. (Most people are quick to say that service has changed—and they are right.) You place your merchandise on the counter, and it's wrapped. The transaction has begun. Now here comes the shift in service. You take out your cash or credit card, hand it to the cashier, and say, "Thank you."

Did you catch that? Probably not! You are thanking someone for *taking* your money. The last time I checked, the *customer* is the one that should be thanked. The customer's job is to say, *"You're welcome!"*

I live in a great home. Do you know who paid for it? The *customer!* I have several cars. Do you know who paid for them? The *customer!* Clothes, education, food—all of these were paid for by the *customer,* and the customer *deserves* to be thanked. Appreciation is a value.

I received a Montblanc pen as a gift from a client. In Harriman, Tennessee, where I live, you can't buy a Montblanc pen. You can buy a Cross pen and pencil and get your name put on it at Chase drugstore downtown. You can buy a box of Bics and Papermates at Wal-Mart. But not a Montblanc. In fact, until I got one as a gift I had never heard of a Montblanc pen. To me, a pen is a pen.

I was flying home from the West Coast and had to change my travel plans and go to Charlotte, North Carolina. When I stepped off the plane I noticed a small kiosk with Montblanc pens on display. I had walked by this kiosk a hundred times, and yet I'd never seen it before.

This phenomenon is called awareness. Before Debra got pregnant I never noticed pregnant women, but when she became pregnant every woman I saw was pregnant—and even some of the men. That's awareness. I always wanted a white SUV. Then when I bought one it seemed that everyone had a white SUV. It's called awareness.

Awareness is to value what glasses are to the nearsighted. Once we see it, we understand.

So I walked up to that Montblanc kiosk because now I had a curiosity. But I also had couth. Couth is a Southern thing, and I am very couthful. I know you don't just ask someone how much something costs. (You think that I made up the word "couthful"? Well, I did. If my president can make up words, so can I.)

I asked the young salesperson if I could get a refill for my pen. I then handed it to her; but she didn't reach out and take it the way she would a pen. No; she held it between the palms of her hand and said in a hushed voice, "Sir, this is not a pen; this is a fine writing instrument."

"Well," I said, "can I get a refill for my fine writing instrument?"

"Sir," she said, "this is a Montblanc Presidential—a limited-edition pen. There were only about 1,100 of them made. That will be $12.95—"

I don't need another pen, I thought. *I already have a pen.*

"—for the refill."

For the *refill?*

Why, I could buy a whole *box* of Bics or Papermates for $12.95! I could get a nice Cross pen for $20. So in a very *couthful* way I asked her what else she could tell me about my pen.

She got the serial number off the cap and asked if I would like to know my pen's lineage.

Right. I'm from the South. I don't even know my own lineage. (That's why we marry our relatives.) But I said, "I would love to know my pen's lineage."

She squinted as she read the tiny print. "Your pen was purchased in Baltimore, Maryland. The customer purchased all 10 pens that we had in the store. Five hundred seventy-five dollars."

I felt faint. "My client paid $575 for 10 pens?"

She shook her head. "No, sir; he paid $575 for *that* pen."

So I owned a $600 pen. Who would have ever thunk it? Let's analyze this: I got a free pen. Why does it have value? Because it is a $600 pen? No! It has value because my client gave it to me. I appreciate the gift; I value the pen.

When my children were small, they always brought home art they had created at school. Where do you think Debra and I hung it? That's right—on the refrigerator. Years later that artwork is still boxed up and guarded like fine art. Time is that kind of gift, too. Only by living it wisely can you increase its value. Next time I see you, Greg, I'm going to do something *just* for you: you have a big hug coming, Bubba! (No; not from Dolly—let that go.)

Greg can't believe how far his life has come in only a few days. He would never have dreamed a week ago that he'd be playing golf with his son, Patrick. And the past week at work had been so encouraging—everyone had been eager to help him succeed, and that success had bolstered his confidence. His workmates had changed somehow, become different . . . No, wait—maybe it wasn't them. Maybe it was him! But how could his attitude have changed all those people at work?

It hadn't.

He grabs an extra pair of socks and puts his car keys in his pocket. Settling into the car seat, he prays, *God, bless this day. Bless my son. Thank You for helping Patrick forgive me. Continue to make me new again each day. Teach me to be an opener. Bless my friend Dale and his family, Father. Thank You for forgiving me and allowing me to be of value to those around me at home, at work, and in my church.*

Turning the key, Greg begins to grin. He has learned how to be thankful. He is becoming an opener.

The day passes much too quickly. Patrick and Greg enjoy lunch at the golf course and play 18 holes of golf (best ball). Laughing and picking at each other is a memory Greg will cherish for a lifetime. After golf they go shopping, then have dinner. At dinner Patrick asks Greg if he'd like to help him cook dinner two nights from now for some of his friends. Greg is happy to be sharing in Patrick's life, and they decide to meet after work at the grocery store in Pearl to pick up supplies for the dinner. Greg drives home with a permanent smile on his face, content and happy that the day has gone so well.

At home he leans back in his office chair to gather his thoughts. Then dropping his feet to the floor, he sends this message to Dale's e-mail:

Lunch and 18 holes of golf—$67.

Wet shoes from getting the ball out of water on the back nine—$45.

Shopping and dinner with Patrick at the mall—$178.

Drive home with the day's memories—priceless!

Eight days ago you asked me to read a can every day and explain to you what I've learned. I have learned so much more than eight lessons. This week, this day, these last hours that I've spent with my son, are all outcomes of the cans. The can is not a container; the can is positively reacting to life's outcomes. By using the can, the opener understands cost (how much we appreciate life) and separates it from worth (how much we value life).

Eight days ago I had no way of knowing where I would be this evening, but I think you did. You knew I didn't need advice—I needed a map to find my way back to me. Eight cans would have been enough, but I'm sure the last two cans will be containers of hope and encouragement as well.

Good night, Dale! Sleep well.

Greg

Dale logs on to his AOL account and reads Greg's e-mail; tears well up in his eyes at the tenderness of his friend's words. Greg isn't the only one who is learning from the cans. Affirmation and appreciation are values of the heart.

"Where are you, honey?" Deb calls out from the hall. "Are you ready for bed?"

"Just a minute, sweetie—I'm finishing some e-mails."

Dale shuts down his computer and walks into the bedroom. Deb looks up from the mirror. "Was that Greg?"

"Yes. He and Patrick played golf today and had some value time."

"You mean quality time, right?"

"Every second of it, honey; every second."

CAN OPENER

A CONFUSING RIDDLE:

TWO FROGS ARE SITTING ON A LOG. ONE DECIDES TO JUMP. HOW MANY FROGS ARE ON THE LOG?

Behold their sitting down, and their rising up; I am their musick.
—*LAMENTATIONS 3:63.*

It is not the sitting but the doing that is music to God's ear.
—*DALE HENRY, LOOSE TRANSLATION.*

When Greg calls Patrick and thanks him for playing golf and invites him to church, he gets a surprise. "Hey, Dad, why don't you go to church with me?" Patrick asks.

Greg's thrilled. "See you there," he says.

He puts down the receiver and grabs a day-old Krispy Kreme doughnut.

Ah, the breakfast of champions, he sighs. Sitting down in his favorite chair, he opens the ninth can. He pulls out the story and begins devouring it and the doughnut at the same time.

C. G. Sexton lives across the street from me in Harriman. You've never met C.G., but I'm positive that you'd admire him. C.G. was in the car business back when you could buy Coca-Cola only in drugstores. You'll never find a man with a higher level of integrity. I love this guy! Debra and I hope that he and his wife, Margie, never move.

I was watching C.G. go to work this morning. (I'm positive he didn't know he was being spied upon.) He always parks his car under a large oak tree by the driveway and lets his wife keep her car in the garage. As he was walking around his car he came face to face with a spiderweb. Well, C.G. did a spider boogie-woogie, flailing his arms around and swiping frantically at his face. Then he started looking for the spider—he looked on his front, then on his back. When he was satisfied that he and the spider were not sharing the same space, he did that little shudder-shake thing, accompanied by a vocalization that sort of sounded like *"Yuck-a-wooo-hoo!"*

Of course, I wouldn't dare let him know that I had witnessed the whole episode. I had seen this kind of behavior before in my own home. When she was little, Lauren didn't like vegetables. Whenever she put vegetables in her mouth, she'd make the same C.G. spider shudder-shake, followed by *"Yuck-a-wooo-hoo!"* I would sometimes have to excuse myself so she couldn't see me laugh.

Life is like that. The more reserved the moment, the more humorous the observation. I guarantee that if you will let most people in on the moment, they will see the hilarity.

I once was having lunch with a tableful of nurses. When our meal arrived, I noticed that everyone was having a vegetarian meal. I personally love vegetables. I was raised in the country—we always had a garden, and my family enjoyed fresh produce at every meal when it was in season. But at the table that day mine was the only meal that was not completely vegetarian—I'm talking about a big juicy steak—and I sensed that every eye at that table was looking at my plate. You know the look—a cross between envy and I-can't-believe-you-are-eating-a-steak.

I knew I needed to ease the tension and defuse the moment, so I looked at all these lovely Florence Nightingales and said, "It's wonderful to see you ladies eating so healthfully—vegetables on every plate! Your mothers would be proud. You should really feel good about yourselves. I just noticed—and I can't believe it—we are *all* vegetarians!"

It was electric. Every woman there wanted to respond to my comment, and I could feel the anxiety beginning to swell. Finally the woman on my right leaned over to me and became the speaker of the group, saying what every person at that table was thinking. "Dr. Henry, you are not a vegetarian!"

Without looking up I said, "Sure I am! I'm just not as committed as the rest of you."

The woman directly across from me tried not to laugh but ended up shooting iced tea out her nose.

A healthy sense of humor, Greg, will keep your life in balance. It's an active ingredient for the opener.

Flying commercially is not fun. Delays and crowds, lost baggage and rude travelers—all add to an already-stressful experience. There's an oasis among all airlines, though. I enjoy flying on Southwest; the fares are a value. But that's not why I like that airline. The seating is open (you don't get a seat, you get a hunting permit). But that's not it, either. Getting your boarding pass is easy, as long as you get it on the Internet 24 hours before your flight. Otherwise, you could end up with an infamous C ticket (as in center seat). But that's not why I like it. Nor is it because the peanuts are good. I'd love to say it's because they give good service—but it's self-service. You don't even have to talk to a single living soul to get on board.

So what makes them different? Well, Southwest is 99.9 percent GOOFY (getting out of flying yuckies). The "flying yuckies" is that uncontrollable feeling that no matter what you do, a travel connection at a hub could go bad. When I fly Southwest, I always fly direct—fewer connections means that you have fewer opportunities to encounter the flying yuckies.

Direct flights to Texas and Florida out of Nashville are common occurrences for me, so I've come to know quite a few of the flight attendants. During a morning flight to Orlando I saw Lisa, who immediately gave me a big hug and asked, "Dr. Dale, would you do me a favor? Would you hand out the peanuts?"

Greg, you're probably wondering why I'd want to hand out peanuts. It's a perk, really, a wonderful opportunity to serve people who serve me all the time, a way of doing something that is out of the ordinary. So at the appropriate time I began handing out peanuts, and I was having a ball. About halfway down the aisle I spotted a gentleman who looked as if he'd lost his last friend. In a sour tone he asked, "You not got anything warm?"

"No," I said, "but I'll put a pack of peanuts in my armpit, and I'll be back when they get toasty."

It turned out that he was a meeting planner from Minneapolis. Since then he's hired me to do several meetings, and every time I work for him I bring him a pack of peanuts.

What happened this spring was even better. On a flight from Nashville to Texas I saw Chip, one of my favorite Southwest flight attendants. (Just thinking about our names makes me smile; you know, Chip and Dale.) As soon as I boarded he grinned at me and asked, "Hey Dr. D, would you do me a great big favor? We're only about half full tonight, so will you do the safety briefing?"

Now, we've all been through the safety briefing on a plane, but do we ever listen to it? Of course not! The reason we don't listen to the briefing is that it's always the same. Mine would not be.

Chip introduced me as if we were at a comedy club. "Folks, on tonight's flight we have one of our favorite frequent fliers: Dr. Dale Henry! He's going to do our safety briefing for us. Give it up for Dr. Dale!"

People good-naturedly clapped and yelled "*Woo-woo-woo!*"

The safety briefing is always done from the front of the plane. But not mine. I ran to the back of the plane and asked everyone to turn around. "Now that everyone is looking this way," I said, "I don't have to point out where the exits are located—you can see them. But should you forget where they are, don't worry, because if we have an accident there will be a gaping hole near you. Don't worry about the exits; just jump out a gaping hole.

"How many of you drive a car that was made before 1960? That's what I thought. That means that *all* of us drive cars that have seat belts. Since we all know how to use them, I'm positive you don't want me to insult your intelligence by demonstrating how to buckle one. However, if you don't know how to buckle a seat belt, please keep yours unbuckled because we've been trying to work you out of the gene pool for some time now."

I was warming to my topic.

"The next part of the briefing comes in two parts. I will do both parts, because they are both equally funny.

"Part one: 'In case of a water landing . . .' Did you catch that? How many of you noticed, while you were waiting for the plane, that there was not one single aircraft on that tarmac that had pontoons? That's right—*there are no pontoons!* So modify that last sentence of the briefing. In case of a water *crash,* your seat cushion turns into a *what?* That's right—it is a flotation device. You knew it was a flotation device when you sat on it, because had it been designed as a seat cushion it would have been comfortable.

"Let's also diagnose the proper way to use the flotation device. Pull the seat bottom to your chest and interlock your wrists. Folks, it's about now that I need to remind you that somewhere between 2,000 and 5,000 people have been sitting on that cushion during its lifetime. Are you *sure* that you want to snuggle up to this cushion when it's wet? I didn't think so. So here's a thought: If we left the cushions in the plane, wouldn't that make the plane float? Yeah, that's what I'm talking about!

"Part two: 'In case of a water evacuation . . .' Let's stop right there. Way before this plane hits the water just about everyone on board, including the pilot, will be having their own personal water evacuation; minutes before we hit the water most of us will already be wet.

"If the plane loses pressurization, Mazola butter tubs will fall from the ceiling. Grab one of them and breathe normally. (You will *not* be breathing normally—you will be sucking oxygen for all you're worth.) Help the child next to you after you have put on your own mask. If the person next to you has been merely *acting* like a child, you can *act* like you're helping them.

"Obey all signs, especially the no smoking signs. No one has smoked on a commercial flight in 30 years, but it's just too much trouble to take those tiny signs off our planes, so we just keep on telling you not to smoke. Oh, yeah; don't smoke in the bathrooms, either. It's easier to put up a smoke detector than it is to take down those little cigarette signs and remove the ashtrays.

"The last part of the briefing is no doubt going to make a lot of you go 'Huh?' In case of an electrical outage—are you ready?—lights will come on on the floor—red ones and white ones. Most of you are thinking *Hey! If my car has an electrical outage, it quits running.* That is exactly right! So what are the lights for, you ask? They are there so we can look at each other's terrified faces, hoping and praying that the pilot will take the energy from these little lightbulbs and restart the engines."

Everyone heard my briefing. I got a standing ovation. Why? Because different isn't necessarily better—unless you take action in a creative way. There's something magnetic about seeing something that is done uniquely. My grandfather's riddle demonstrates this well:

Two frogs are sitting on a log.

One frog decides to jump.

How many frogs are sitting on the log?

Answer: Two!

If you decide to do something different but don't take action, you haven't moved. Practice opening opportunities—don't be an observer. Openers are user-friendly action takers. Keep moving forward, Greg. That way, in case of a water evacuation you aren't just floating in one spot—you're swimming toward the goal.

Greg places the empty ninth can in the box. Patrick and all the people at work were responding to things they observed that were different. It was great to be seeing opportunities instead of obstacles! He grabs another doughnut and looks in the mirror. "Greg Little, you're looking good, my man—looking good and feeling good!" he says to the image grinning back at him. "Working out agrees with you!"

He dresses for church and his rendezvous with Patrick. Patrick is waiting for him, and they go in and worship together. After church they visit with Greg's mother. She too notices a difference in her son, and it does her heart good to see him happy. As he backs out of Patrick's driveway, Patrick waves to his dad and reminds him that they're to meet at 6:00 tomorrow at the grocery store.

Home again, Greg logs on to the computer a little before 9:00:

C.G. sounds like a great neighbor, Dale. C.G. has a great neighbor!

Patrick told me things today that he's never shared with me before. I found myself listening, laughing, and reloving my son. We visited my mother, and she seemed like her old self. It was wonderful!

These are all experiences that I would have missed without your guidance, Dale. Here's what I've learned from the can: Life provides many trails among which I, the opener, may choose. The trip becomes an adventure when I take that first step.

Greg pulls out his Bible and studies for a while before going to bed. As he turns out the light he reflects over the past three days.

WHAT HAVE I LEARNED SO FAR?

- **Can Opener 7:** The opener uses discretion—speaking and listening, communicating and disseminating. By using the can, the opener gains wisdom and integrity.

- **Can Opener 8:** By using the can, the opener understands *cost* (how much we appreciate life) and separates it from *worth* (how much we value life).

- **Can Opener 9:** Life provides many trails among which I, the opener, may choose. The trip becomes an adventure when I take that first step.

CAN OPENER **10**

OPENER MASTERY:

WHEN IT COMES TO LEARNING,
THE EYES ARE BETTER THAN THE EARS

I will instruct thee and teach thee in the way which thou shalt go; I will guide thee with mine eye. —*PSALM 32:8.*

When it comes to instruction, the eyes have it.
—*DALE HENRY, LOOSE TRANSLATION.*

For Greg, independence is on the way. Things are starting to realign themselves, and the transitions in his life are about to come to fruition. He will soon realize that change cannot be altered—transition, however, can be mastered as long as we use the can to become the opener. Greg will never forget his tenth can.

Greg stretches off the night's sleep and walks into the kitchen for his morning coffee. "What's this?" he mutters. "My coffeemaker must be on the fritz." He shrugs. This is the best excuse he's had in a long time to go out for a cup of joe.

He opens can 10, but instead of taking out the contents he brings can and all with him to the coffee shop. As he begins to empty the can, he's momentarily interrupted when an older gentleman behind him speaks up.

"I've seen people read books, magazines, and the newspaper in coffee shops, but I don't think I've ever seen someone read from a can."

As Greg turns, he recognizes an old friend. "Ray! How are you doing?"

Mr. Ritter adjusts his glasses. "Greg? Greg Little, is that you? I didn't recognize you with that gray hair. What are you doing these days?"

The two catch up on old times. Then the older man's curiosity can be contained no longer. "So what's in the can?"

Greg smiles. "A friend is mentoring me."

"Must be valuable advice if you're carrying it around in a can!"

Greg explains the 10 cans, and how he's working on becoming an opener. Mr. Ritter pulls his chair closer, interested. "What a great concept! So how are the lessons coming?"

Greg shares all the concepts he's learned during the past nine days.

"Wait a minute! I thought you said there were 10 cans."

"I'm just getting ready to read can 10," Greg explains.

"Well, I don't mean to disturb you. I just couldn't believe it was you when I saw you come in! Before I go, though, I wonder if you'd be interested in interviewing for a position that's going to be available with our company in a week or so. You're close to retiring from the state, right? I could use someone with your experience and positive attitude."

Greg grins broadly. "Yes! That sounds great."

Mr. Ritter gives him his business card and waves goodbye. "Call my secretary today," he says. " You need to hop on it—the job won't last long."

"Don't worry; jumping is my specialty!" Greg says.

Then, opening can 10, he sits back and begins to read.

Greg, the Renaissance Esmeralda Resort in Indian Wells, California, has it all figured out when it comes to making you feel welcome. On the floor of all the elevators are carpets that have a different message for each day of the week. Unless you know to look, you'll never see it. I've been welcomed to a hotel in many ways, but putting the message on the floor got my attention.

Everyone knows about elevator etiquette. You're taught from an early age that you don't talk in the elevator. The eyes are to face forward, keeping a sharp focus on the numbers. When someone enters, you politely nod your head. If you have to talk, it must be done in low tones. Should you get off on the wrong floor, never go back in the same elevator, because it shows your fellow elevatorians that you are clearly not versed in proper procedure. We learn about elevator riding by watching others. The senses are great teachers because they help us to determine when things are right or wrong.

When our girls were small, I once needed to rent a van for a trip we were taking. Just before I left to pick it up, Debra instructed me to be sure to get a nonsmoking van. So I informed the gentleman at the rental place that a nonsmoking van would be the only thing I would rent.

Arrangements made, I climbed in and headed for home. The van smelled as if it had been freshly cleaned. Unfortunately, though, the longer I drove it, the more the van's true nature—or true smell—became obvious. It was a smoker. I knew Debra and the girls would not be pleased.

So I stopped at a car wash and invested 75 cents in baby powder spray. I lathered it on, spraying every square inch of upholstery and carpet until the van smelled like the nursery at the hospital. I was very pleased with myself.

I parked the van in the driveway where it would be handy to load. As it began to warm up in the afternoon heat the interior's true underlying aroma reared its ugly head. LeAnne, the first one in the van, took one sniff and said, "Daddy, it smells like babies have been smoking in this van."

It was a long drive back to the car rental place at the airport.

When my girls were growing up, I told them two stories, from time to time, one of which contained a lie. Let's see if you can find it:

Story one: Girls, your daddy loves you very much, and I've had fun growing up with you. You and your mommy have taught me so very much about little girls. Daddy never grew up with little girls, you know, so the three of you have had to teach me about Barbie pretend, tea parties, and dress-up. I've always felt as if I was in the learning mode, looking and observing before I did things so that I wouldn't commit a playtime faux pas.

Your mother is the expert, though, when it comes to children and the things you need to shape each of you into young girls. Dad just knows when to pick up a new refrigerator box when the old playhouse starts to wear out and get smelly. I've enjoyed every second of my education in early childhood, and if I could, I'd keep you small forever! Nothing makes your daddy feel more loved than when you two cuddle in my lap and tell me that you love me.

So I want you to know in advance that you'll grow up and you'll become teenagers. You'll cross over from childhood to adolescence someday, and that's when your daddy will become the expert. I've spent most of my life with teenagers, and I've been studying their rituals and mores. Girls, when you become teenagers, Daddy will have to teach Mommy the new rules of car driving freedom and telephone usury frequency.

Story two: *Girls, when you become teenagers you'll most likely start looking at boys a little differently. You'll want to talk to them and hang around them (nasty creatures that they are), because you'll think they are interesting. Then you'll want to go on dates. Daddy is real excited about that! (Note: There's the lie!)*

So when you start dating, and boys come to get you to take you out, Daddy wants to meet them too, so that he can get to know them better. Anyone you think is nice, Daddy will think is wonderful—and I want to tell them so. So before you girls go on your first date I will be there to meet and greet your new friends.

Both of those little girls looked at me with sparkles in their eyes and fell for it hook, line, and sinker.

Have you noticed, Greg, that there's an atmosphere that hangs over a house when there's been an altercation? Dogs are the first to notice. Our dog, Sandy, always runs up to me and wiggles all over when I come home. However, several years ago I found myself in the middle of an anger management seminar.

I came home after four days to find Sandy curled up in her bed in the corner of the kitchen. There was no wiggly greeting. I didn't know I could read a dog's mind, but it sure seemed that she was sending me telepathic signals: *People aren't happy here, so why don't you come over here and lie down with me, because these people aren't bothering me.*

My child bride was standing in the middle of the kitchen floor, balancing a quarter on her thumb. I knew nothing good could come from this. She asked me to call it in the air, and I yelled, "Heads!"

Catching it and looking at it closely, she announced, "You lose!"

"What did I lose?"

Debra frowned. "You are teaching your daughter how to drive!"

So it had all come to this. Debra was losing her babies, and I was gaining teenagers.

LeAnne had turned 15, learning-to-drive age, and I was ecstatic. I told Debra that I was all over it and dug out the keys to the 1978 Jeep Cherokee. Every man on the planet knows why I chose the Jeep Cherokee: it was worth $200.

OK, the Jeep Cherokee has *some* redeeming qualities: it sits up high, offers good visibility, has great maneuverability, and is an off-road vehicle, just in case. The *real* genius behind my choice, though, lay in what was *between* the front seats: *the emergency brake!* If you have the emergency brake in your hand, you have control. You can stop the car whenever and wherever you choose. You dah *man!* I've always wondered how LeAnne felt when she climbed up in that Cherokee for the first time, and there was her daddy, his hand on the emergency brake, clicking the button nervously again and again.

Keith Steelman was the first teenage boy who took one of my girls out. I was so excited! I went right up to my office and got on the Internet. After several minutes of research I printed out my findings and put them in my desk drawer. When Keith arrived, he was as nervous as a cat in a room full of rocking chairs. Choking on every word, he said, "You wanted to see me, Dr. Henry?"

"Yes, Keith; come in and sit down," I said, waving him toward an old ladder-back chair that my dad had given me. One of the legs had been broken off, so I sawed the other legs off so they would all match. There is no way a human being, let alone a teenager, could be comfortable sitting in that chair.

Keith sat down.

"Tell me a little about yourself, Keith." I felt like a defense attorney with a handful of evidence, grilling a guilty defendant.

"Well, you know my family—we all go to church together."

"Yes; Boyd and Carol are wonderful folks. You have a sister, right, Keith?"

"That's right, Dr. Henry; she's my baby sister."

"Do you love your baby sister, Keith?"

"Of course I love my sister!"

"Keith, if someone were to hurt your sister, Kelly, what would you do, son?"

Keith sat up straight and looked at me for the first time. "If someone hurt my sister, I'm afraid I'd do something I might be ashamed of later."

I liked this kid. I stood up. "That's good, Keith. I like it when a young man understands responsibility. That's why I'm sure you'll understand when I tell you that if something happens to LeAnne while you two are out, they will never find your body, son."

I pulled the research from my desk drawer that outlined how to dispose of human bodies and showed him. He thought it was interesting.

"Keith, it is my sincere desire that you and LeAnne have a wonderful time. But I need you to know that I expect her to return to me in exactly the same condition that she left. Are we clear on that?"

"Yes, sir," Keith said.

"Do you know what the curfew is?"

"Yes, Dr. Henry. Mrs. Henry said we had to be home by 11:00."

I clucked my tongue sadly. "Keith, that is Mrs. Henry's personal curfew time. What do you think mine might be?"

Keith reflected for a moment. "I'm thinking closer to 10:30."

"That's good. Now, Keith, you two have a good time. You might want to go down to the living room. LeAnne will be ready soon."

I knew LeAnne wasn't going to be ready; she's like her mother. He'd have to cool his heels at least another 15 minutes. That gave me time to go downstairs and get a spent shotgun shell. Folding down the ends, I put a piece of double-sided tape on the shell and slipped outside to mount it on the dashboard of his truck.

Keith walked LeAnne to the truck and opened the door for her. Boys know when something has been done to their truck. He spotted the shotgun shell right away. I was on the front porch, watching them, and I shouted out, "Keith, anything in your truck that wasn't there when you got here, son?"

"Yes, sir."

"Can you see it, Keith?"

"Yes, sir."

"If you mess up, son, you won't see the next one."

A little more than a year ago Keith asked for LeAnne's hand in marriage. Several months from now I'll get to call him son. And it will make me proud.

We have a little ritual at the Henry hacienda. Every Friday or Saturday night we do pizza and a movie, depending upon my travel plans. After pizza, we play cards. If you want to know what your kids are doing, play cards with them. They'll tell you everything while they're playing—they forget you are their parents. The secret is that you can't look as if you're shocked when they tell you something you didn't know. Just smile and say, *"Weeellll, now; how interesting!"* Then when you get to your bedroom later you can go half crazy with worry. (Hey, don't tell my dad we play cards, Greg—he's a Baptist deacon, and Baptists believe card playing can lead to premarital dancing.)

It was pizza night again. I went by LeAnne's bedroom and called out,

"LeAnne, you want to drive down and get the pizza and a movie?"

"Sure, Dad; I'll get ready," she blasted back from her bedroom.

Now for some more Henry home insights. I cannot go into my own home, the home where I live, take my car keys from my trousers, and put them on my wife's furniture. I don't *have* any furniture. Dale Henry has a bowl—single, solitary, white, cheap, ceramic bowl—in which to keep his keys. (Even my dog has two bowls.) I cannot put my bowl on my wife's furniture. It lives on top of the highboy.

This night, instead of grabbing the 1978 Jeep Cherokee keys from my bowl, I picked up the keys to the 1982 Mercedes-Benz 380 convertible, Daddy's pride and joy. My head said, *Put those keys back in the bowl right now!* My heart said, *It is metal and glass, rubber and leather; a lifeless and feeling-less possession—but it would make her day.*

I carried the keys into the living room and tossed them to LeAnne. She knew the second the keys hit her hand that they weren't the keys to the Jeep Cherokee.

"Dad, wrong keys!" she said.

"No, baby girl," I said, "we're going to drive the Mercedes tonight."

She looked at the keys in her hand again, then said, "I need to change clothes!"

"OK. Toss the keys back to me, and I'll let down the top."

What went into that bedroom that night was an adolescent child—baggy sweatpants, baggy sweatshirt, and a baseball cap with her hair tucked up underneath. What came out of the back of my house was Vanity Fair. She was wearing a sundress, and her hair was pulled back. There was makeup on her face and high-heeled shoes and nylons on her feet that reminded me of when she used to play dress-up. This stunningly beautiful young woman was the spitting image of her mama.

She jumped into that Mercedes and drove it off that mountain as if she'd been born to drive it. When she stopped at Highway 27, where we turn right to get our pizza and a movie, a small hand reached across the console of the Mercedes. "Thanks, Dad," she said.

Every dad who has ever taught his daughter to drive knows what happened next. I looked like C.G. Sexton in the middle of a spiderweb. Fidgeting and fumbling, I was going through all kinds of gyrations before blurting, "Oh, honey, it's just a car, and you need all kinds of experience driving different automobiles."

LeAnne looked at me in puzzled shock. "No, Daddy; I love driving your car. It's the coolest thing I've ever done! I was thanking you for not putting your hand on the parking brake."

Funny. She was right. Here was a car worth thousands of times more than the Jeep Cherokee, and I had no need to control.

The next part of this story isn't to impress you, Greg, or to make you feel like Dale Henry is some kind of cool guy. It is merely a story about a dad and a daughter on a short drive on a beautiful fall day.

As we turned right on Highway 27 a funeral procession was approaching about 2,000 yards in front of us. In the South we honor and value someone who has had a great loss. Whenever my grandfather met a funeral procession, he always pulled his car to the side of the road, got out, and put his Stetson hat over his heart and stood respectfully until every car had passed. My grandmother, Dad, and Mother did the same thing. I know; I've seen them do it. I can't remember once hearing my parents say, "Hey, we're in a hurry today—no time to stop." We just did it.

And I do it too. I'm not just teaching LeAnne how to drive; I'm giving her the rules of the road. And some of them aren't in the Tennessee driver's manual; they're in our hearts. I leaned over to tell LeAnne why her daddy always pulls over when a funeral procession passes. I filled my head with thoughts and my lungs with air, ready to begin expounding—but it was never said. LeAnne had pulled over and gotten out. And we stood side by side on that glorious fall day, and not a word passed between us as those 51 cars passed by.

My head was a whirl. Why did she do that? Why had she stopped? I hadn't told her to.

She stopped because I had always stopped.

Very few people will listen to instruction or be mentored by someone who teaches lessons in a vacuum. It is easy to say do good, treat people fairly, have a high level of integrity, and lead with passion. But the eye is a much better student than the ear. If you want those around you to put on the mantle of leadership and transition, you have to show them how it fits. You have to demonstrate with your actions the desires of your heart, and then no matter what barriers you face, they will see the opener in you.

Carry the can in your heart, and your body will follow.

Ten cans. Ten lessons. Ten parables in 10 days. How can such small things make such big changes? Greg thinks. *Change is an outside force that we feel obliged to let control our life. Transition, on the other hand, is manufactured from within, directing us with past experiences toward becoming better.*

His cell phone rings. It's Dale.

"Hey, Greg! Has it happened yet?"

Greg smiles. "Has what happened yet?"

"Did you get it? Has it sunk in?"

"I think so, Dale. The can is our positive way of dealing with events over which we have no control. The opener is who we become when we seize those moments in life and use them to lead others through their personal changes. The leader is not changed because of transition; the leader is transitioned by change to show others how to lead."

"Is the eighteenth going to be all right with you?"

"What's happening on the eighteenth, Dale?"

"That's when you and I, and Patrick and my new son-in-law, Brandon, are going to tear up the golf course in Jackson, Mississippi."

"Hey, Dale, I, uh—"

"Yes, Greg?"

"I love you, brother; and thanks for the gift."

"Don't try to soften me up—Brandon and I are going to give you and Patrick some golf lessons."

He laughs happily. "We'll talk at breakfast on the eighteenth. Let me see if I remember right—you're buying?"

"Yes. Go ahead and rub it in; I'm buying."

"Later."

Greg slides into his car and goes to work for the last time. He calls Mr. Ritter's office and schedules an interview. Work wasn't work today. Being at work was a joy.

When 5:00 rolls around, he calls Patrick. "What time do you want to meet at the grocery store?"

"I'll see you there in about 15 minutes, Dad."

"See you then, son."

It's a sunny day at the Bush bean plant in Tennessee. Ten ordinary cans

of chili beans roll off the conveyor belt on their way to a grocery store in Jackson, Mississippi. When they arrive, they are carefully placed on the shelf.

"The guys are usually pretty hungry. You think chili is a good idea? We should put in a ton of meat—they like meat. Growing boys, you know ... Ah, there they are now. Let's see ... Ten cans should be enough, don't you think so, Dad?"

"Yes, Patrick; 10 cans should be plenty."

THE TEN CANS

CAN OPENER 1:

Openers find avenues where others find dead ends.

CAN OPENER 2:

Openers tell everyone their passion—shared excitement energizes the can.

CAN OPENER 3:

Openers understand that team members are happier, more optimistic, and better problem solvers when the opener is happy, optimistic, and a problem solver.

CAN OPENER 4:

Openers use the transmission of the can by working inside remission and transition.

CAN OPENER 5:

Openers know that the vessel is cleansed only when the lid of self-doubt is destroyed.

CAN OPENER 6:

Openers should never get out of whack. Instead, they put people back in whack by opening cans.

CAN OPENER 7:

Openers use discretion—speaking and listening, communicating and disseminating. By using the can, the opener gains wisdom and integrity.

CAN OPENER 8:

Openers understand *cost* (how much we appreciate life) and separate it from *worth* (how much we value life).

CAN OPENER 9:

Openers may choose among the many trails that life provides. The trip becomes an adventure when the opener takes that first step.

CAN OPENER 10:

Openers know that the can is their positive way of dealing with events over which they have no control. The opener is who they become when they seize those moments in life and use them to lead others through their personal changes. The leader is not changed because of transition—the leader is transitioned by change to show others how to lead.

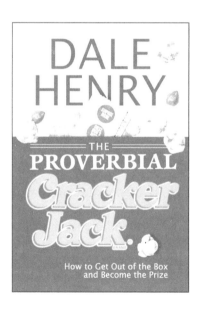